With Best Wish
from,
Brenda Howlett-Nye

Finding Me

Common Sense and a
Little Ingenuity Prevails

BRENDA HOWLETT-NYE

© Brenda Howlett-Nye, 2015

Published by Brenda Howlett-Nye

A CIP catalogue record for this book is available from the British Library.

ISBN 978-0-9934935-0-8

Book layout and cover design by Clare Brayshaw

Prepared and printed by:

York Publishing Services Ltd
64 Hallfield Road
Layerthorpe
York YO31 7ZQ

Tel: 01904 431213

Website: www.yps-publishing.co.uk

Contents

Poems

Family Tree for Brenda Howlett Mason

CHAPTER I

Early Days

I burst into the world on 20th April 1933 at a healthy 6½ pounds bundle of joy, despite the traumas of economic recession and my Mother having been very ill with whooping cough during my development. I was, according to family narrative, a happy, healthy child and as this book will tell destined for a life of trials and tribulations intermittently beset with times of joy and happiness. So began my life with my Mother, Father and sister in our modest 1920s semi-detached at 20 Hilltop Road in leafy Reigate, in the beautiful county of Surrey. Our house was one of twenty-two, built in a semi-circle with a pretty shrubbery in the centre.

My Father William was a worthy son of St Andrew's in the ancient Kingdom of Fife, Scotland and soon became known to the good citizens of Reigate as Jock, an epithet that remained with him until his dying day. While serving as a Constable in the Reigate Borough Police he met my Mother Eva while conveying important messages to her Father, who was no less than the Chief Inspector of his Division. Captivated by her attractive dark hair, soulful eyes and demure demeanour, he left nothing to chance and they married in 1928.

My sister Yvonne was four years older than me. We were very different in many ways; she had beautiful dark curly hair and mine was fair, fine and straight. My Mother described it as being like "A yard of pump water"!

My earliest memories are when my sister and I went into hospital to have our tonsils and adenoids out when I was just three years old. The operation was common practice in those days, almost routine. I remember being pushed along on a trolley to the operating theatre, wearing long

1

white stockings. The orderly pushing the trolley chatted to me, trying to put me at ease and keep me calm; he had a kind, friendly, smiling face. I do not remember any more until after the operation, when I awoke to find myself in a high sided cot, in a ward surrounded by other children.

I remember screaming when a very grumpy nurse came with a drink. I jogged the cot; the drink shot right out of her hand all over the bed clothes. I found her very scary and created such a scene! She was not amused, so pushed me in my cot into a bathroom until I became quiet. To this day, I can see that bathroom; there was an oblong window high up near the ceiling. Although I was very frightened I was also very angry. What seemed like hours later, I was taken back into the ward and moved next to my sister. She became very perturbed when the little boy next to her, with whom she had become friends, was moved down the ward to make room for my cot; she definitely did not want me next to her! Later that year we were invited to the hospital Christmas Party, I went into a grotto where Father Christmas was handing out gifts. He gave me a little torch. I was so thrilled; I treasured it for years.

I remember my sister had a beautiful china doll, which was almost sacred to her. I was never allowed to touch it. One day when I was around four years old and Yvonne had gone to school, I thought I would play with it while no-one was looking. What harm could that do? I carefully lifted her out of her little cot, and was carrying it into the kitchen when disaster struck; I tripped on the doorstep and as I fell, the doll smashed and shattered into a thousand pieces. I remember feeling so afraid and thinking "she will kill me"! My Mother scolded me and I waited with trepidation for my sister's return home from school. That evening her rebuke was delivered when she told me that during the night "**THE BLOOD WILL RUN**"! I was frightened to go to sleep, but I was so relieved to find I had actually made it through the night when I awoke the following morning.

I can remember my mother pushing me in a pushchair to visit my grandparents, who lived about four miles away. We used to pass a church and outside were twelve trees which were supposed to represent the twelve apostles. She would pick me a leaf to hold. It kept me quiet until we reached my grandparents' house. My grandfather kept chickens and racing pigeons. He had a moustache which always prickled when I gave him a kiss. My grandmother made delicious cucumber sandwiches and lovely golden buns. They had a dear old spaniel dog named Trudge, who slobbered a lot and had rather a strong odour.

I can remember going on holidays, travelling to my father's family home in Scotland, my father proudly at the wheel of his old Austin Seven. My sister and I used to take it in turns to sleep on the back seat or curl up on the floor, where if you stretched out there was a big hump in the middle through which the main drive shaft went. On one of these occasions I can just remember we camped on a farm, and while helping my father pitch the tent, my Mother was stung by a bee. The weather turned cold so we went to the cinema to warm up and my father took my shoes and socks off. I remember him warming my feet in his hands while we watched Snow White and the Seven Dwarfs.

We had a wireless with a large separate loud speaker; the interior was made from a type of cardboard with a wooden surround. I could not figure out how it worked – I thought there must be little people inside. As there was a tiny crack at the bottom, I forced it open a little bit more. I still could not see anyone, so I pressed a little harder and it tore. My mother came in, and she scolded me when she saw what I had done, saying "Just wait until your father comes home!" I sat petrified, waiting for him to return. When he heard the whole story, he was amused that I was so intrigued and explained in simple language how it all worked. There were no little people inside.

I started school at five years old and can still visualise myself with my father sitting outside Lesbourne Lands School waiting until it was time to go in. We had just two classrooms. Several of the pupils came from one family, they had originated from Newcastle. Twenty-five of them lived in one house. They all spoke with a strong accent and often had quite a strong smell too, and nobody was keen to sit next to them! We used to give them our clothes when we had grown out of them. The school nurse used to come round regularly to check us all for head lice, nits and fleas.

My mother was one of eight children and very family oriented. The whole family used to get together on high days and holidays and aunts, uncles and cousins used to play good old fashioned parlour games. Consequences, I think was the favourite, where we all wrote a girl's name on a piece of paper, folded it over, then passed it on and continued likewise with a boy's name: where they met, where they went, he said to her, then she said to him, and finally what the consequence was. In the end, rather bizarre stories, often very amusing and some quite risqué, would be read out. "Squeak piggy squeak", was another favourite. We took it in turns to be blindfolded, then went round the room and had to guess who we were sitting on, having asked them first to give a squeak. We had to be turned around three times to disorientate us while everyone else swapped seats.

My mother never went back on her word, so I always knew where I was with her. She often quoted sayings that her parents had taught her, such as "Never let your left hand know what your right hand is doing", "Never do business with friends.", "Red sky at night, shepherd's delight; red sky in the morning, shepherd's warning", and dozens of others. If I had been very disobedient she would say, "Mark my words, God will punish you." In case he might have been watching, I can remember picking my nose under the bed clothes so he couldn't see.

My father was one of a family of ten, quite strict, but I usually managed to get round him. He hated to see any food wasted. My mother sometimes used to stew damsons for pudding. When sugar was rationed, they were so sour they used to make me come out in goose pimples and it felt like my hair was standing up on end. My father used to say in his Scottish accent, "You'll eeet it," so I had to sit at the table until I had finished it, or anything else I did not like. I remember having to fetch a strap that he kept in a drawer in the kitchen for when my sister or I had been very naughty. It was then laid on the table beside me just to make sure I did, "Eeet it", or do as I was told.

I used to spend a lot of time with Mr. and Mrs. Hattin who lived six doors away from us and had no children. Mrs. Hattin had been a cook. She taught me how to make mint sauce by chopping the fresh mint up with sugar before putting the vinegar on, and many other useful tips.

They had two little Pekinese dogs; Bill who was rather bad tempered and Tessie, who I loved. I was allowed to nurse her on my lap, provided that I sat quietly while the cooking was in process. Bill resented my presence, so we treated one another with mutual respect.

For my seventh birthday, Mr and Mrs Hattin gave me one of my most memorable birthday presents. I received a small briefcase with my initials engraved on the front. It looked so important. I went home elated, heralding, "I've got a real briefcase and it has a "bu", a "hu", a "mu" AND a keeeey!" I kept it for years with my most treasured possessions locked safely away inside.

Mr. Hattin worked at the bus station. My sister and I used to call him "tease pot" as he loved to tease, but never in an unkind way. Sometimes he was a little confused when pronouncing words and I remember when my Mother told him we had a new electric water heater fitted, he said that he was also thinking of having one of those "emotional" heaters fitted too!

I used to play with two little boys who, like me, lived in Hilltop Road. We were much the same age. One day Tony showed Michael and me how to dip our biscuits in sand and eat them. I hasten to add that it was not something that became a habit with me. He also suggested it would be a good idea to play at being Gypsies and go round our road begging. Some of the neighbours gave us biscuits and sweets and things were looking up until we knocked on the door of an old lady, who asked us if our mothers knew what we were doing. We were forced to terminate that brilliant idea immediately, fearful that she would let the cat out of the bag.

The milk was delivered daily from The Jersey Dairies, by horse and cart. If the milkman spent too long chatting to a customer, one of the horses used to pull the cart across the pavement to investigate any edible vegetation that he could find, growing over the next door neighbours' fence. He would be forgiven should he leave a large deposit of manure in return; it would quickly be shoveled up by the neighbours, as a treat for their roses.

My Mother's cousin, Ben Beadle, used to call round once a week with a horse and wagon to deliver household necessities and other hardware.

A rag and bone man, shabbily dressed, used to come round pushing a cart, calling out in a monotonous tone, now and again, "Any old rags and bones!". Every evening at dusk, a man on a bike would arrive with a long pole to turn on three lights, which were fixed to a huge, high ventilation pipe in the centre of the grassy patch in the middle of our cul-de-sac. It lit up the whole circle.

When I was seven, just before we were evacuated to Scotland, I was playing with the girl next door, in the woods behind our houses. We were sitting on a stile which prevented the cattle from getting into the woods but was still part of a right of way which led into a lane at the bottom of our road. A man in a raincoat came along and sat on the stile too. He asked us if we would like to go into the wood to play manoeuvres. We had been taught never to speak to strangers so were about to leave, when he opened up his raincoat and asked, "Have you ever seen such a beauty as this?" It was truly outstanding (as well as upstanding!) and enormously larger than the one a little boy had shown me from under the tablecloth while having tea and cakes at the Sunday School party earlier that year. We knew it was definitely time to go and shot off home as fast as we could.

The girl from next door was older than I was and told me not to tell anybody, but being a policeman's daughter I knew it was wrong and it should be reported, so I went straight home and told my mother who contacted the police. I was whisked away in a police car to the police station where I was shown pages of passport photographs of men. They asked me lots of questions and wrote down what I said. They were able to trace the man and later that year he appeared in court. My statement was read out as, "He stuck out his sausage." My father, on returning home having attended the hearing, said to me that if it ever happened again it would be better to say he exposed himself. Fortunately that never became necessary in my formative years!

Thinking back, I recall having to wear knitted vests; they really made me itch, especially when wearing a liberty bodice over the top in cold weather. Little girls didn't wear trousers until the war when it became more practical for girls to wear siren suits, ready to dive into often cold, damp, air-raid shelters.

CHAPTER 2

Wartime Memories

In September 1939, after many rumours and much speculation, World War Two finally broke out. I was six years old and on holiday with my parents and sister in St. Andrew's, Scotland. We had to return home a few days early. I could sense an air of uneasiness from the adults as no one knew what lay ahead. We said emotional goodbyes to our Scottish relations and journeyed south, back to Reigate in Surrey.

My Father, who was in the Reigate Borough Police, was too old to join one of the Services so was commissioned to form an Auxiliary Ambulance Service for Reigate and Redhill; they were known as the A.R.P. (Air Raid Precautions). Having trained in his youth as an engineer, he was able to arrange for the conversion into ambulances of several second hand powerful, somewhat expensive cars, such as Bentleys and other classic vehicles.

Every able bodied person had to contribute something for the War Effort. Young men of eighteen and over had been called up to join the forces. If they were declared unfit for the forces, they had to work on the land or contribute in some way depending on their capabilities. Older men, if they weren't Wardens, joined the Home Guard which was like a local army. Ladies who held a driving licence had to learn to drive the ambulances. They were given instruction by my father, along with first aid lessons on how to deal with casualties. Many other women joined the W.V.S. (Women's Voluntary Service), others went to work in munitions factories. Younger, stronger girls joined The Women's Land Army.

Much disruption was caused when iron railings were requisitioned for the war effort. I remember some being torn down from a place called The Wilderness, which was on the way to my grandmother's house. Air raid shelters were dug out so people could shelter underground from the bombs, and gas masks were fitted. Newspapers displayed grim stories and pictures of European atrocities, swastikas and many of Hitler in the form of cartoons mocking him. Sticky paper was stuck in criss-cross patterns on windows to stop the glass from shattering and blackout curtains had to be made for all windows as no light was allowed to be seen from the outside. Air raid wardens would patrol the streets at night to make sure the rules were adhered to. If a glimmer of light was showing, a man in a tin hat would tap on the door and warn the occupants, in order that they remain hidden from enemy aircraft, especially in built up areas.

Nothing much happened over the first few months, and then almost overnight things changed dramatically. The sirens began to wail in the most blood curdling way to warn everyone to dive for shelter as an enemy bombing raid was imminent.

Red warnings would come by telephone to my Father if he was off duty. He would leave and soon after we could be sure the sirens would sound. I remember our phone number was Reigate 3543; if I was nearest to the phone and had to answer it, that was the number I had to recite.

Our air-raid shelter was under the garage and doubled up as a workshop. My Father had dug it out and reinforced it with concrete. We spent many hours down there contemplating our fate.

On one occasion, when we were running for shelter, I remember hesitating before going down the steps, to watch what was known as a Dog Fight. An enemy bomber was being attacked by one of our fighter planes. It shot round diving up under the big plane, shooting at its undercarriage. Suddenly, a plume of black smoke billowed out from the tail of the bomber as it spiraled out of control, whereupon I too spiraled down the steps before an explosion echoed in the distance. It was a great relief when the eerie note of the all-clear sounded and we wearily traipsed back into daylight. When the sun was shining the whole situation seemed almost unreal, and it was hard to believe it was really happening.

Food was rationed; posters were up everywhere saying, "Dig for Victory". Lawns were dug up and vegetables planted. Chickens were kept where possible, their rations supplemented by any household scraps. Once they stopped laying they were then eaten, along with the young cockerels.

Pig-bins were also distributed for waste food, which was collected and boiled up, then sold on to pig farmers. This waste became known as "Tottenham Puddings". They did resemble huge puddings, weighing around 20 kilos each. As well as all kitchen waste, it was not unusual to find spoons, knives, forks and other household utensils that had accidentally found their way into the bins. The pigs played with them in their troughs until they were retrieved.

Sadly many ships bringing food in from abroad were sunk, torpedoed by submarines or bombed by enemy aircraft, so non-essentials like oranges and bananas were seldom seen. If they did manage to get through, long queues formed and people stood patiently waiting to be served. I remember on one occasion I had to queue for ages when a consignment of oranges had arrived at our local greengrocers. I fainted, and while flat out on the pavement someone brought me a glass of water from the chemist shop next door. The following day I came out in a rash; it was measles.

Obesity was almost unknown. Our rations had been carefully calculated for nutritional benefit, so although meagre by today's standard, they kept us from starving. Our weekly allowance was 8oz of cheese, 4oz of butter, 12oz of sugar, 4oz of bacon, 6oz of meat and 2oz of tea, one egg and egg powder that was edible when soaked into bread and fried with any dripping fat that had been left over from the meat ration. The milk ration was a quarter of a pint a day for adults and half a pint for children.

Petrol, coal, soap and clothing were also rationed and black market activity was rife. People who had dealings with contraband goods were known as spivs. They had ways, fair or foul, to acquire rationed goods to sell on at a profit.

I recall my mother in tears when bread became rationed. I used to swap my sweet ration with my grandmother, in exchange for her sugar allowance, so I could sweeten my tea. Pots were scraped clean, not a morsel was wasted.

Soap was conserved by sticking the last tiny sliver on to the next bar. We had one bath a week in the recommended five inches of water, followed by clean clothes. Washing was usually done on a Monday by hand, boiled in a copper first, rinsed then wrung out by turning a handle on a mangle, often a child's job, while mother fed the wet articles through. Then they were hung outside on a clothes line, propped up with a wooden pole, to dry in the wind and sun. This routine was somewhat disrupted when the air-raids were at their height.

My mother collected for the Red Cross. She visited all our neighbours once a week and sometimes I accompanied her. I enjoyed meeting everyone and listening to their latest happenings. There was great camaraderie; everyone pulled together and helped each other throughout the difficult times.

During 1940-1941 what became known as the Blitz started in earnest. London and other big cities were bombed incessantly night after night. My father would be called out to organise the ambulances and join the team of wardens, Home Guard, WVS and nurses rescuing the injured and devastated people whose homes had been destroyed.

I used to wince when the gruesome details came to light in the news the next morning, and sense the emotion by the grim looks and hushed tones of the adults commiserating with one another.

Anti-aircraft guns were situated in strategic positions and searchlights beamed light high up into the sky, enabling the gun crews to locate bombers coming over and shoot them down. The noise from the guns was quite scary as it was not easy to differentiate between the guns and the bombs at seven years of age. I used to curl up with a cushion over my head to dull the noise when a gun situated in a field nearby was firing. My heart became quite used to fluttering.

One evening, when we had been visiting my grandmother's for tea, my Father came to fetch us in an ambulance, having had prior warning that an air raid was imminent. I remember sitting in the back and looking out towards London. The sky was lit up by an ominous red glow, London was ablaze. A deluge of cluster bombs had been released showering incendiary devices down, causing fire on impact. Stirrup pumps had been distributed in all buildings in case of fire, but had little effect on such massive onslaughts. Fireman had difficulty coping. Thousands of people were killed. Buildings were reduced to rubble, due to the continuous bombing night after night over many of our big cities up and down the country.

The Prime Minister, Winston Churchill, broadcast over the wireless, encouraging the nation to be strong, chin up and keep calm and carry on.

There was of course no television in those days, so the wireless was our main source of news. King George VI and the Queen also used to tour the ruins playing their part in keeping Britain great.

In 1940 the British Expeditionary Forces, together with the French Army and Canadian troops that had been aiding the defence of France, were forced to retreat and were trapped in coastal areas of Northern France. This prompted the extraordinary rescue operation known as the Dunkirk Evacuation, when naval vessels, working alongside hundreds of fishing boats, small leisure craft and lifeboats went across the Channel to help rescue the trapped soldiers, many of whom were injured. The very famous operation was code-named Operation Dynamo and also became known as the Miracle of Dunkirk. It was truly a miracle; between May 27th and June 4th over 338,000 troops were rescued.

At the bottom of my grandmother's garden was a railway line. I used to stand on the fence with my sister and cousins watching and waving to train loads of wounded soldiers, all dressed in blue uniforms with white shirts and red ties, some of them waving back and throwing coins to us. In a corner behind the railway line my grandfather kept his chickens, also some pigeons that were bred for racing. They had won many cups and prizes and they too played their part in helping to win the war. They were frequently taken over on board aircraft flying across the channel on their missions, where our spies put secret coded messages in tiny containers on their legs. Then they were released and flew home. My grandfather, as a trusted, retired police inspector, was responsible for taking the messages to a secret place, known only to a few. It was the headquarters of the South Eastern Command and was operating deep in caves under Reigate Hill. It was said that Churchill, Field Marshall Montgomery and other important dignatories had attended secret meetings there.

As the blitz started and bombs were dropping all around, my father decided that my mother, sister and I should be evacuated to his relations in Scotland, so it was goodbye to Reigate for a while. I can remember my mother telling me that Hitler liked Scottish people. I really believed her and I thought that if the Germans invaded, we would be ok.

My Father came to London to see us off, but before we could reach the main terminal, there was an air raid. The sirens wailed and everyone dived for cover in the nearest underground station. It was an awesome sight. It was packed full of terrified people, some still sleeping down there following an earlier raid. When the all clear sounded, relieved crowds emerged like ants on a mission from the bowels of the earth into bright sunlight.

Fortunately, we managed to locate a taxi to take us to the main station for our departure; this meant a brief tour across London, an experience I will never forget. The devastation that met our eyes on the way was horrendous. So many buildings were demolished as part of the rescue operation. Some were in ruins and there was rubble everywhere. We saw firsthand what the Blitz had done and was still doing. The whole scene is still etched in my memory. Squads of men in tin hats were sifting through the rubble in a stoical, systematic manner, helping to rescue the victims. The ingenuity and resilience of people in those dark days was truly amazing.

We reached the station with time to spare, so my father took me to see the powerful steam engine that was quietly puffing clouds of black smoke into the air. It was the famous Flying Scotsman, waiting patiently to spirit us away to safer, more tranquil surroundings. We said another tearful goodbye to my dad.

The journey seemed to last forever. However we arrived the next morning and were met by Father's relations. My Father had five brothers and three sisters so we had numerous aunts, uncles and cousins, plus a Swiss grandmother and a Scottish grandfather.

School in St. Andrews was quite a shock compared to Lesbourne Lands, my little infant's school in Reigate. St. Andrews had an excellent educational system. The West Infants was a kindergarten. I attended the East Infants, which was for seven to eleven year olds. It was still known as The Fishers' School, as the children of fishermen went there in the past. The Borough School was for eleven to fourteen year olds. Brighter students then went on to The Madras College, and from there had the opportunity to make it into the famous St. Andrews University. The Fishers School was near the harbour, with the castle and the famous Royal and Ancient golf course nearby. The ancient cathedral ruins were just the other side of the playground. Mine sweepers could often be spotted in the distance from the classroom windows, sweeping in the North Sea.

The winter of 1941 was exceptionally cold – the sea actually froze and a dead whale was washed up on the sands and caused quite a commotion. Girls were allowed to wear trousers, known as Siren Suits, to keep warm.

St. Andrew's is steeped in history which we had to learn, with particular attention paid to the battles that the Scots won. Because I was English, they would point at me chanting with glee that they had beaten us on those occasions. Teachers were very strict and a leather strap with thongs on the end lay on the teacher's desk as a reminder to us all as to what the outcome would be if we chose to misbehave. I learned to join up my writing and all my times tables backwards and forwards, so instilled I can still remember them to this day.

That winter I had an abscess in my ear and was quite ill. A doctor visited the house. He prescribed M and B tablets which cleared up the infection but left me deaf for a while. Antibiotics were not available. At school we were tested every week, and sat in order of merit through the class. The most diligent sat top left at the back, then less and less so with each row down. After my ear infection I was disheartened to find myself down to the front row. However after a week or two I managed to achieve the back row again.

I soon became accustomed to the routine, walking to school through the main South Street, often past clusters of Polish soldiers who were stationed nearby. They were very friendly and many stayed on after the war. Before I reached the school, I had to pass the cathedral ruins, which was a bit creepy as it was supposed to be haunted in places. The crypt of the cathedral, under part of the ancient ruins is where we had to go if there was an air raid – quite an experience. Raids were few and far between but one night an enemy bomber was chased out over the North Sea by planes from Leuchars, an air force base not far away. It dropped its bombs on the way and one landed at the bottom of the garden of the house where we were staying, causing much excitement.

After a while my mother rented a flat near our relations and at weekends I used to play with my cousins and visit my grandparents. My grandmother used to make the most delicious soup, perhaps with a little too much pepper, but it warmed us up. I recall sitting in front of the fire on a stool with a bowl of steaming hot broth, where a large cuckoo clock with the cuckoo popping out now and again would mark the time.

The flat where we stayed had a brewery yard with stables behind it. I spent time watching the huge dray horses being fed. They pulled the wagons that delivered ale to the pubs. One was called Prince, a lighter type of horse that had won many cups and prizes. At weekends and evenings, we played in the brewery yard. Sometimes if we were very lucky we would find a missed bottle of lemonade. Some of the older boys used to smoke sticks of cinnamon and on one occasion, a boy caught his shoe alight. I also recollect watching with horror as another little monster dissected an unfortunate spider by pulling its legs off in a basin of water. I often wonder if he became a surgeon.

At the end of 1941, the enemy bombing eased off a little, as the Germans turned their attention more to Eastern Europe and Russia. During the respite my Father thought it would be safe for us to return home. To earn the fare my mother, sister and I went potato picking. Children were given time off school to help. It was hard work, and I remember crying one day because I was so cold and wet. However we earned enough money to pay for the fare home.

CHAPTER 3

St. John's School

I was 8 years old when we came back from Scotland. It was fun to be home again. It seemed strange at first but I tried to settle down at my new school which was St. John's, at Redhill in Surrey. During my time in St. Andrews I had acquired a strong Scottish accent which left many of the local children quite bemused; gradually this disappeared. When we had history lessons, we learned about the battles the English had won, so again I was taunted. There still seemed to be a big rivalry between the Scottish and the English.

When I first came back from Scotland I came top of the class of forty-two, beating Fleur Adcock by half a mark. Unfortunately, I seemed to go steadily downhill academically, as I found it difficult to adjust to the contrasting teaching methods. Fleur Adcock however went on to become a famous writer and received an OBE in later life!

At St. John's, I clashed with Miss White the headmistress from the first month I was there. Later in Mrs. Barrett's class, we were given stars to encourage good work and black spots for the reverse. One term I ended up with more black spots than stars and I remember Mrs. Barrett saying, "Brenda Mason I suppose you are proud of your black spots." I returned her sarcasm by saying, "I thought they looked more striking than stars." It did not go down well!

My first teacher at St John's was a pleasant young mistress who was, coincidentally, married to a Scotsman from St Andrews. She was off sick one morning, so Miss White, the head mistress took over her duties. I had been at the school for less than a month when Miss White gave me a note to carry to all the teachers to sign. I was quite honoured that this errand had been bestowed upon me. I managed to negotiate all the classrooms successfully, an achievement considering it was the first time I had ventured into them. I found all the teachers, who signed the document as I requested. Mission accomplished. I handed the paper over to Miss White, receiving just a grunt. I went back to my desk.

When I had sat down, there was some maths on the blackboard that I could not understand, as it was very different from the maths I had learned in Scotland. I had missed the introduction to the lesson so I sat with my hand up to ask for some advice. Miss White glared at me a couple of times but otherwise completely ignored me, so I whispered to the girl next to me asking for information. Miss White noticed instantly and the next thing I heard was, "Brenda Mason come out here." I went out to her desk, and was reprimanded for talking in class and told to go and stand outside the door. I felt this was a totally unjust command and refused to go. I did not want to be seen standing outside in the hall, where the class doing PE out there would be gawping at me. She took hold of my wrists to put me out, whereupon I struggled, pummeling my fists into her well endowed bosom. Although I was crying, I felt satisfied that justice had been achieved when, with a very red face and a quivering top lip, Miss White told me to go and sit down. She never forgot or forgave me, so we were locked in battle on and off for the rest of my time at St. John's school.

There was more conflict when I retrieved my tennis ball. Just above the main door was a flat roof not far from the staff room window. Every now and again the caretaker would bring a ladder and climb up to throw down balls that had landed up on the roof. On one unfortunate occasion mine went up there and I didn't want to wait so, as there was a drainpipe coming down from the roof beside the door, I thought it would be quite simple to retrieve my ball. With a lift from friends to help me up to the first joint of the pipe, I managed to shin up the rest of the way. There were several balls already up there so I enthusiastically threw them down. Feeling jubilant that all had gone so well, I was dismayed to find Miss White standing, lip quivering once more at the door as I climbed back down. Oh dear, it was "Brenda Mason" again – more lines to write! I became quite adept at this by holding two pencils between my fingers, it cut the time it took to write them dramatically.

Another incident occurred when ready cooked dinners had just become available. They were delivered mid-morning and left inside the main door, beside the staff room steps. Several of us were dying to know what was for dinner, so I dared to look. I just happened to be peeping in the note book on top of the heated cabinet, to see what was on the menu, when I found that Miss White had crept down the stairs and I was caught red handed. It was, "Brenda Mason," yet again. For a while I had to sit in a desk facing the wall so as not to disrupt the class.

Miss White always took us for needlework. On one occasion my ball of pale blue wool accidentally rolled into the inkwell and turned into navy blue. Miss White was not amused. The final encounter came when we all had to make ourselves a dress. I chose one that had smocking at the top. Every time we had finished a task we had to take it out to Miss White to be examined. I had spent ages carefully sewing the most exquisite, diminutive stitches for the smocking. When I had finished, I took it to Miss White for approval. She looked at them and with a derisive glare said, "What are these? Tacking stitches? " and took hold of the loose end of the thread and ripped them all out, and triumphantly told me to, "Do them again."

My encounters with Miss White are the first things that come – or maybe leap – to my mind, when I recall my time at St John's school.

As the seasons changed so did our games activities. We played hop-scotch and ball games in winter. I was in the netball and rounders team, and sometimes we were lucky when we played other schools and were invited to stay for tea. In the Spring we had skipping and hoola-hoops, marbles in the Summer with leapfrog a popular pastime too. For swimming lessons we used to walk through Redhill town to the swimming baths, which were almost opposite the sports ground. In the Autumn the boys liked to play conkers, looking for the best and the biggest as they dropped from the trees. School sports took place on a field just a short walk from the school.

In the early days I had to walk the two miles to St. John's school, two miles back for lunch, back again in the afternoon and back again at the end of the day. If I was late for school, my excuse was that I had forgotten my gas mask. Later we were able to buy dinners at school, so after we had eaten, we played on Redhill common, often looking for the long strips of silver foil which our planes had dropped to interfere with enemy radar. Swapping shrapnel was mostly a boy's hobby.

We did not have much to do with the boy's school. They were taught quite separately but on St. George's day, their head master would conduct a service in the playground. We would all congregate and he would stand up on a large box to conduct us. We sang patriotic songs such as Land of Hope and Glory, I Vow to Thee My Country and Jerusalem and finish with God Save The King. Once, to our amusement, Mr. Bennett toppled off his box. After the service we all had half a day off.

Little boys from an orphanage, which I think was in the village of Meadvale, attended our infants school and some of us older girls used to befriend them at playtime. They were poor, sad little souls dressed in grey and wearing heavy hob nailed boots. Very often they had gentian violet dabbed on their faces against a skin disease called Impetigo.

Those of us who were keen on gardening were allowed a tiny plot up by the wall in the playground. I shared mine with another girl and we grew some flowers. On one occasion her mother had made us some bread pudding from stale bread and we left it by our plot on a stone wall, saving it for a mid morning snack. Alas, when we came to eat it, a whole nest of ants had invaded the paper bag containing the pudding we were so looking forward to. It's not easy sharing with ants!

Towards the end of my time at St. Johns school, we had cookery classes. We had to walk to Hooley School, near Redhill and stayed for the day.

We were taught by Miss Thrupp about nutrition and how to eat sensibly with the aid of symbols, for example a brick indicated food that contained protein for building muscles, and a petrol pump illustrated food high in carbohydrates for energy. Pictures of fruit and vegetables showed food with high vitamin and mineral properties.

Miss Thrupp also taught us how to wash hairbrushes and combs and the correct way to wash different fabrics; cotton and other delicate fabrics such as wool and silk, and how to hang them on the washing line for the wind to blow through them. We learned how to iron clothes and even how to fold them correctly – nighties into three and shirts into two. Embroidery had to be ironed on the wrong side first.

We had to scrub the tables at the end of the day and boil our dishcloths. The highlight of the day was when we hung them out to dry on the railings by the boys' playground. We always tried to time it for when they were having their break!

CHAPTER 4

Evacuation to Wales

In 1943 when I was ten, strange, ominous rockets, which became known as doodlebugs, began to plague the south of England. They were rockets that looked like planes, with jets of smoke spurting out from under their tails. They made the most menacing, intermittent drone as they flew overhead. Finally when their engines cut out, they crashed down with a mighty explosion, causing immense destruction. I remember seeing one flying almost overhead as we scrambled down the steps into the gloomy, damp, air raid shelter at St. John's school. Barrage balloons, situated on open ground near the outskirts of Redhill, prevented many of the doodlebugs reaching the heavily built up areas nearer to London, which was their intended destination. It was a very frightening time, especially at night when I was trying to sleep, lying absolutely petrified, listening to the drone, praying that the engine did not cut out close to us.

We were living in a danger zone and therefore parents were advised that it would be safer for children to be evacuated. Preparations were made. Parents were given a list of the necessary items to pack. It was a highly emotional time. Nothing was certain but we did know that we were going to Wales. Younger children had to accompany the eldest. My sister was four years older than me, so I had to go with her school, which was Reigate County School. On the day of departure we assembled in the County School grounds where we had identification labels tied to our lapels. After all the tearful goodbyes we traipsed off with our belongings to Reigate railway station.

An enormously long train pulled by a huge steam engine destined for Wales, stood belching out black smoke and a smut landed in my sister's eye as we were about to board. I remember looking out of the window on the way as we went along, watching the rear carriages still snaking round the bends like a giant caterpillar, completely packed, the atmosphere tense with excited children.

When we arrived at Bridgend we were herded into a dark, dingy hall, where we were ordered to strip off behind some dilapidated blue screens, to be examined for signs of fleas and lice because the consignment of children before us had come from blitzed London and had arrived complete with livestock attached! After the examination we sat and patiently waited, while we were all found accommodation. To me this felt rather like being auctioned off in Redhill cattle market.

It was compulsory for anyone with a spare room to take in evacuees. The single children were billeted first. Many of the boys found homes on farms, where they would be useful. My sister and I were among the last to go and were taken to a mining cottage in Abberkenfig. The motherly lady who received us welcomed us with open arms. She had a heart of gold. When we went inside, it came as a bit of a shock – we felt we had stepped back in time. There was just a tap above a drain in the kitchen which was very different to what we were accustomed to. All the neighbours from the adjoining row of cottages were invited in to view the new evacuees. They were unanimous in assuring us that we would be, "Very appy eer," in their strong Welsh accent.

When it came to resting our weary heads, upstairs we were confronted with yet another shock. When the door creaked open, there stood a very ancient double bed with a giant sized chamber pot underneath, strategically placed on a vile smelling rush mat. Light and fresh air wafted in through a broken window and holding up a chair, in place of its missing leg, sat a huge, dilapidated family Bible.

My sister and I had never slept together in the same bed, and as a consequence, a state of war broke out when I encroached her half of the mattress, which felt like the Himalayas. It caved in with a mighty ravine in the centre. Peace was restored by stuffing a lumpy pillow down the middle, to separate the top half of the bed. A good kick ensured feet didn't stray across the ravine down at the bottom.

The next day we met some of the other children who had been billeted nearby to swap notes on our latest experiences. My sister's friend was staying near the village green. She gave us a vivid description of how the master of the house had arrived home drunk.

A few days later, our billet was deemed unsuitable so Mrs. Mills, the WRVS lady who had delivered us, came and picked my sister and me up in her very impressive car. Feeling like royalty, we then cruised back to her rather more palatial house, on the main road leading into Bridgend, where we were given temporary accommodation. We realised our luck had changed for the better, when we were given the elegant guest room. I became friendly with the maid called Elena. She used to let me feed a stray feral cat she had befriended and christened Kitty-puss. It used to come every morning for its breakfast, outside on the kitchen window sill. Sometimes I was sent shopping and bought edible seaweed called laver, considered a great delicacy, and we ate it for breakfast. I also had to purchase expensive fish, some varieties of which I had never seen or tasted before. Fish was plentiful being near the sea.

Mr. Mills was a kindly man; he was something to do with the coal mining around Port Talbot. He sat quietly reading his paper and would occasionally chat to me. Once he took us to the pictures. He allowed me to grow some radishes in his garden and I was thrilled when they were ready to eat and we had them for tea. Mrs. Mills' mother had rooms in the house. She was elderly and had a speech impediment so she was difficult to understand but she used to happily shuffle about around the house. Mrs. Mills was always very busy with her WRVS work.

Soon after our arrival in Wales I started school at the Pen-y-bont School in Bridgend. I do not remember learning much, except about the battles the Welsh had won. Some of the lessons were conducted in Welsh, so I didn't understand a word. I was the only evacuee from our group attending the school. I felt like a fish out of water. However, I did learn to sing Land of My Fathers in Welsh, because we sang it at the end of every afternoon before we went home.

I used to help Elena sometimes, for example drying the dishes and putting things away. The larder was a very interesting place to investigate. Hanging from a hook as I went in the door was a specially cured whole leg of ham. It used to grow a fur coat of mould on the outside. One evening we were allowed to stay up and dine with some visitors. The supper was specially laid out. Seeing ham slices delicately arranged on a beautiful china plate, I enquired if it was some of that mouldy ham from the larder, whereby I received a hefty kick under the table from my sister, followed by a lull in the scintillating conversation.

A vicar's daughter had been billeted next door to us. She used to sit on the adjoining wall, discussing the facts of life with my sister; being four years younger I found all the facts most intriguing. Further enhancement of my education came when I met another evacuee whose sister, like mine, went to the Reigate County School. Being a similar age, we had much in common. Her father was an undertaker. I sat next to her on a coach trip one day, but all memories of the actual destination are long forgotten, contrary to the conversation on the journey which was such a memorable and enlightening one. I learned from her somewhat lurid account, complete with graphic and gruesome details, what happens to us after our demise.

After a while another billet was found for us, with a grumpy, retired school teacher whose house was creepy, cold, dark, dingy and most depressing. A massive slag heap loomed up at the end of the road. The school teacher slowly showed us round, saying she hoped we were quiet little girls. I guessed the "Should be seen and not heard" type of child was what she had been hoping for. I'd seen enough and realised that I had to do something quickly, and resorted to crying. She didn't approve and deemed us unmanageable, so we were rejected on the spot and happily went back to stay with Mrs. Mills for the rest of our time in Wales.

We had to go to church three times on Sundays. I thought once would have been quite sufficient, as we had to walk there and back. At weekends there were various gatherings in the park near our billet. Once, it was a gymkhana; there were horses of all shapes and sizes participating. I was in my element and watched with interest as they took some of them down to the stream to paddle, drink and cool off.

Backing on to the park was the kitchen of a bakery shop. On hot days the top door was left open and the wonderful smell of newly baked bread and cakes wafted out into the air. It was interesting to watch all that was going on inside. I was intrigued by the man who made the doughnuts and smoked as he kneaded a large lump of dough. He never took the cigarette out of his mouth and as the ash grew longer it finally dropped off and was incorporated into the mixture. I was mesmerised by this, so waited to see if the next bit did the same, which it did! Further along the road, I would stop to buy some sweets. An elderly lady sat huddled in a dark corner of her shop waiting for customers; also in that dark corner, was a spittoon. She had a wonderfully accurate aim.

Some weekends, if the weather was fine we went to Porthcawl, which was by the sea. There was a big funfair there and we used to look for coins that had accidentally been dropped around the various stalls, then we could have a go on some of the rides. We went swimming too.

Ogmore-by-Sea was over six miles away. We used to walk there, taking a short cut across the fields, through a picturesque village called Merthyr-mawr. We precariously negotiated our way over two sets of stepping stones, past the ruins of Candleston Castle, then over more fields to the sea. It was a long way but worth it. Once there, we watched American soldiers as they practiced driving huge trucks, called Ducks into the sea. When the wheels were out of their depth they became boats. It was fascinating to watch, as they drove a long way out before returning. We didn't know it then, but they were preparing to cross over to France for D-day.

One day, on the way home from one of our treks to Ogmore, my sister was really hassling and goading me to hurry as it was getting late. Half way home in the middle of a large field I was absolutely exhausted and decided I'd had enough, so I lay down and refused to move any further. My sister strode on until she disappeared from sight. I was tired and very angry with her. Shortly afterwards she re-appeared, having trudged all the way back to find me. After her pleading and gentle persuasion in a more affable tone of voice, I condescended to rise and follow her all the way back to Bridgend. She has never forgotten or forgiven me for the incident! Another memorable time, we had a confrontation in our bedroom, when a chair I wielded in self defence narrowly missed going through the window, but most of the time we were impeccably behaved!

Our parents managed to come down once to visit us. It was great to see them again. Shortly afterwards, the V1 and the more deadly V2 Doodle-bug rocket bases were bombed and my parents considered it was reasonably safe to go home. It was time to go back to St. John's School.

CHAPTER 5

From Hartswood to Cromwell Road and Sheephatch

It took a little while to re-adjust to the routine back at St. John's school. Air-raids became few and far between and eventually petered out. Here in the south of England there was a massive build up of army and air force activity. We used to watch convoys of troops in all types of army vehicles trundling through Reigate town on the way to the coast. At the same time, night after night, squadrons of our planes would drone overhead, fully loaded with bombs. They would return early the following morning, with gaps in their formations, many having been shot down over enemy territory. Others would be spluttering, still airborne, limping back to base.

D-Day had been meticulously planned and it was obvious to everyone for some time before that a major turning point in the War was imminent. It finally came to fruition, when the navy and our troops made a surprise strike across the English Channel and started to re-patriate France. The Russians attacked the enemy from Eastern Europe. The Americans also helped us, and on 8th May 1945, World War 2 ended. There were terrific celebrations for Victory in Europe (VE) Day. There were street parties everywhere. Our reserved little cul-de-sac held a party on the green, in the centre of our road. Later that evening, my father took us up to the top of the tower of the Reigate Municipal Buildings, where we gazed at all the lights turned full on. Once again, Reigate Town sparkled at night, for the first time since the war had begun.

A few weeks later the war with Japan ended abruptly when two Atom Bombs were dropped, with catastrophic consequences, causing appalling loss of life, leaving thousands severely maimed. Although people celebrated, it was a sad and poignant time for everyone who had lost loved ones on both sides. Wars seem so utterly banal, yet they continue through the centuries.

While I was growing up, I had many friends from very diverse backgrounds, some were quite posh, others came from less fortunate, rather more frugal backgrounds. I happily mixed with them all and tended to copy the way they spoke. I especially enjoyed mimicking the London and Cockney accents and using 'Cockney Slang'. I remember my mother saying with a look of disgust, "If only you could hear yourself; it's degrading and you sound so uncouth"!

If I brought friends home, my father used to quiz them with, "Where do you live? How long have you lived there? What does your father do? How many brothers and sisters do you have?" He usually stopped short just before asking them what they'd had for breakfast!

I first met Ena, my lifelong friend, when she joined our class at St. John's school, at the age of eleven and we soon became firm friends. She lived on a farm on the Hartswood Estate which her father farmed. My father knew her parents, so I was allowed to cycle the four miles to Hartswood and spent many memorable, happy hours with her and her family, engaging in many mischievous deeds. She had an older brother called William, her younger sister, Mary and a much younger brother, called Henry. To reach the back door at Ena's, I had to flatten myself against the wall of the house and sidle along, trying to avoid the large dog who appeared to have a voracious appetite for human flesh as he leapt to the end of his chain, lurching towards all strangers with his top lip raised and teeth glistening.

One of the first exciting encounters on the farm was watching Ena trying to balance in circus style on a pony. Speckles the pony was not used to being ridden as her job was to pull a trap for her owner, the Lady of Hartswood Manor. However, Ena had other ideas and although she managed to sit on Speckles and stay on with difficulty between bucks, it was a very different matter when I tried. I came straight off with the first huge buck. Ena, determined not to be beaten, finally managed to train her to go forward while she stood up, balancing on Speckle's backside and rode her round as though she was on a circus pony.

We used to play hide and seek in and out of the farm buildings, up in the hay lofts and in the barns. There was an old tramp who lived in one of the outbuildings. I was told he had fleas and lice so I gave him a wide berth.

In the summer we used to swim in the River Mole, which flowed through the farm. There was an old boat that leaked like a colander. We used to take it up the river, bailing out the water as fast as it seeped in through the bottom. It was a job to keep it afloat.

On one occasion, when we had been swimming, we left most of our clothes on the bank. When it was time to go home, we returned to find that our clothes had disappeared. Ena's younger brother Henry had hidden them, which was not funny as we were in a hurry.

Sometimes I stayed for a delicious meal. The whole family, including Uncle John, sat round the table chatting about the latest happenings. They all had a wonderful sense of humour and a lot of leg pulling went on. I used to love the way we cleaned our plates with bread ready for the pudding, to save the washing up. Their poor mother was always on the go, she seldom seemed to sit down. She used to make the most delicious marrow and ginger jam and one day Mary asked if I would like to lick the spoon when she was clearing the table before washing the dishes. Of course I said, "Yes," as she waved the spoon in the air, she then popped it in my mouth. It was covered in mustard and was the cause of much amusement.

They were the first people I knew who had a television and I can remember a programme which came on with a cartoon character called Hank. He was a cowboy and the programme always started with him riding in saying, "Howdee neighbours!"

Henry was very good at amusing himself. When he was about four years old he used to sit quietly playing under the table. When we went to get up, we discovered that he had been busily linking us all together by tying our ankles with string. When it was harvesting time, Henry was able to steer the little Ferguson tractor round the field, enabling us to pick up stooks of corn. He used to jam his foot on and off the clutch, nearly shooting those on board off the trailer.

William used to line up tin cans on a wall and we would shoot them off with his air gun.

When any of the youngsters had been naughty and their mother was trying to find them, they would hide where the ferrets were kept and wait a while for her to disappear before they emerged, as she had a strong aversion to ferrets and their smell.

At harvesting time, there was always a chance to increase the meat ration. When the last cut in the middle of a field came to the end, it was always full of unfortunate rabbits who had sought sanctuary in the tall corn. It was like a massacre. They were quickly put out of their misery, gutted and one hind leg was slit and the other one pushed through. They were then strung onto poles, to make it easy for two people to carry them home. Rabbit pie was on the menu around the district. One interesting fact was that all male rabbits die with both front feet straight and all female rabbits cross their front legs. It shows up when they are strung up on the poles. The same principle applies to live humans; when walking in snow females leave just a single track and males leave two. It's surprising what one learns down on the farm.

One day we were climbing up an elm tree. It was one of an avenue that led to the manor house. Going up quite high was fine until the wind started to blow and the whole tree swayed. It was frightening trying to negotiate branches to climb down. Risking life and limb, we were relieved when we finally made it down in one piece.

We made a swing high up in the barn where they stored potatoes, and were swinging away merrily when it broke. We were bruised and so were the potatoes.

One day when we were down at the stables a big thunderstorm blew up. Neither Ena nor I liked thunder storms so William had to come and rescue us. Another day the cart horses cleverly opened a gate onto the circular green in front of the manor house. They cavorted all over it with their huge feet. We had to stamp in all the divots.

A few years later, after the Lady of the Manor had passed away, the manor house stood empty for a while and one evening, five of us played hide and seek all over the spooky manor house, creeping up the huge staircase to the bedrooms to hide in wardrobes and cupboards, also venturing down into the wine cellar, which was dark and quite scary!

I remember one afternoon Ena had to leave class early to go home and help out with the milking. Labour was short just after the war. She left school a few days after her 14th birthday, which was in December. Ena had a beautiful singing voice and left us all spellbound when she sang a solo, "Silent Night, Holy Night," at the end of term concert.

Ena took over the cart horses when she left school. I remember helping her one Sunday evening. She asked me to take Ginger for a walk up to the woods and back, while she prepared his supper and mucked out the stable. They usually had a rest on Sundays so he was quite frisky. Once up to the wood we turned around. To my horror he took off with me hanging on the leading rein for grim death. Trying to control a powerful animal, who knew it was supper time was very difficult. Ena had a wicked sense of humour! She knew that he would give a spectacular performance.

I felt very happy and content when sitting up behind the horse drawn hay rake, with one of her huge horses plodding dutifully along, needing little guidance while rowing up the new mown hay, ready for her brother William to load on to his tractor and trailer and take it back to the Rick-yard, where it was built into haystacks, that were later thatched with straw to keep them waterproof, until the hay was required to feed the stock in Winter.

In 1947 St. John's School became a junior school for children up to eleven years old. As I was then thirteen, I had to leave and go to Cromwell Road School in Redhill. It was a long walk. The school was in a built up area, and the smell of hides being processed wafted over from the nearby tannery whenever the wind blew from that direction. I became a prefect and was given the task of keeping order on the many stairs. I cannot remember learning much there. After dinner we used to spend the rest of the hour going round the shops, finally calling in at the popular bakery by the school for one of their famous jam puffs.

In 1948 some of us had the opportunity to go to Sheephatch. This was a school built by the Canadians especially for children who had experienced a disruptive time in the war. I was so lucky to be given the chance to go there and jumped at the opportunity. It was a wonderful experience. The school was in the village of Tilford, between Guildford and Farnham in Surrey. The buildings were well planned and consisted of beautifully built timber cabins. There were blocks of dormitories for the girls and for the boys, a large main hall, lots of classrooms, a sick bay, and a massive playing field. There was also a large garden where our vegetables grew. In charge was a wonderful headmaster called Mr. Gould, and assisting him a specially picked band of teachers. The staff there were fantastic.

We were all up early every morning, and anybody who dared to flout any of the rules had to run round the huge playing field a couple of times before breakfast, or more, depending on the severity of the misdemeanor. The food was good and after breakfast we had to make our beds, army style, with all the blankets folded up neatly, and lockers tidied. We then stood beside our bunk beds awaiting Mr. Gould's inspection. We all had to be clean and tidy, smartly dressed, with hair shining and well groomed, also finger nails had to be immaculate. Then it was time for lessons. There was a rota for cleaning. Two of us would stay back to sweep damp disinfected sand over the floor to freshen up our dormitories each day.

If the weather was fine and sunny Mr. Gould would arrange trips out and he said that we could do our lessons in the evening. As a consequence we visited many places of interest in the area. They included Guildford Cathedral, Haslemere Museum, Waverly Abbey ruins and several potteries; we also had picnics at Frensham Ponds and treks to Crooksbury Hill to pick berries. We did cross country running and occasionally went to a site where they were excavating for Roman remains. Once a week we went shopping in Farnham.

The Long Walks

We pack our food with greatest care,
our bread and milk we always share.
At last we're all prepared to start,
when some of us have to depart.
Because we have not changed our shoes,
Mr. Grant then gets the blues.
The time folk take is so pathetic,
when all are feeling energetic.
We start at last, and walk quite fast,
time, it seems is flying past.
We puff and blow to climb up hills,
then down the other side, past mills

till as we round a bend we see,
that well known landmark, Crooksbury.
So being fairly near Sheephatch,
we look out for a grassy patch,
for now the ramblers tea time's here,
and soon the packs will disappear.
Tea tastes delicious picnic style,
the bread just vanishes by the pile.
When we've finished pack we must,
with the burdens we're quite just.
We share them round for all to carry,
and then push off, no time to tarry.
The sun has set and cool the air,
we walk along without a care,
although we're weary now it's true,
still we are gay and happy too.
At last we reach our Sheephatch dear,
and walkers know that there's no fear
of sleeplessness or dreams of home.
Oh no, we'll dream of hikes to Rome.

Written in the Spring of 1948 for
The Sheephatch School Magazine at the age of 14 years.

Lessons were fun; Science and Biology were made very interesting. The boys also learnt to cook and press their trousers and the girls could do woodwork and pottery. One of our masters had been in the SAS. He taught us to map read and many other fascinating survival tips. In the evenings, there were various clubs and we could choose which ones we would like to join. I chose theatrical make-up for the shows we put on and joined the Smallholders Club which was run by the headmaster's wife. I learnt the correct way to set a broody hen on fertilised eggs, to produce chicks. We also learnt how to keep laying hens and how to kill, pluck, draw, truss and cook them ready for eating. We also had rabbits and Iris a goat, with her little kid. All sports were catered for and the staff often played too. The swimming pool was open in the warm weather.

The Staff Football Match

The staff turned out one afternoon,
and to the boys great was the boon,
for they had come to play football,
teachers short and teachers tall.
The gentlemen were dressed in shorts
and all of them looked good at sports.
Their legs were bare about the knees
and so they felt a gentle breeze.
At three o'clock the kick off came,
it soon became a furious game.
The staff played hard with craft and skill,
with many a charge and many a spill.
Alas! All good things have to end.
There was no energy left to spend.
With staff on top by eight to one,
thus ended all the sport and fun.

*Written for The Sheephatch Magazine in Summer 1948,
my last term at school.*

The Saturday Evening Hop was very popular. We learnt to do old time dances, like The Progressive Barn Dance, The Gay Gordons and the Old-Time Waltz, to name a few. The event was conducted in a correct manner, presumably to teach us how to behave at social occasions. At the end of each dance the boys had to take the girls back to their seats and give a little bow.

Every opportunity was turned into a learning process. One day someone hoisted a pair of pyjamas up the flag pole instead of the Union Jack. Pupils had to try the culprit as though it was in a real court. They were memorable days.

I was then fifteen and it was the end of my school days. When I was about to leave school, Mrs Gould knew I was absolutely cut out for farming and persuaded my parents to let me follow that course, much against my Mother's will – she had planned that I should become a secretary. To aid my quest to go into farming, Mrs. Gould also persuaded my Father that

I should keep a goat, and to my joy he agreed. He converted a shed and made a door into the wood at the back of our house, an ideal place to tether her. I left Sheephatch with a dear little baby goat I christened Bambi. She grew into a large animal complete with horns and later supplied us, and half the road, with milk. Rationing continued on into the 1950s.

With hindsight, the University of Life is where I learnt most during my formative years. Having a passion for animals and plants, I did achieve my ambition to work with animals and farming.

When I grew older, I still used to visit Ena and her family at Hartswood Manor on my days off, or between jobs. The family had a gramophone, and we spent many memorable evenings playing records and listening to music. Slim Whitman's latest records were always our favourites.

CHAPTER 6

Starting Work

In the summer of 1948 I left school to start work. I was fifteen and the halcyon days playing in the woods at the back of our house with my friends were over.

I remember well my first day at work. My father cycled with me the four miles to Stumblehole Farm at Leigh, near Reigate, Surrey. I was going to work with pedigree Jersey milking cows, and Father handed me over to Peggy, who was in charge of the herd.

The going was very tough, cycling every morning at the crack of dawn, doing a hard day's work and then cycling home again in the evening. I found it extremely exhausting. I think my mother was hoping that I would change my mind about going into farming and become a secretary or at least something a little more genteel – and cleaner! She had an aversion to wellington boots being parked outside the back door, reeking of silage and slurry.

As the days shortened and the weather turned cold and wet, it was arranged that I lodge with Peggy's parents, the farm manager and his wife. The family came from Norfolk and I was fascinated by their accents. Peggy's mother used to finish many of her sentences with "eh, it's a rum-un ain't it," especially if the outcome of a situation was unknown. She reared the pheasants that were later released in the woods of the estate ready for the shooting season. She was also a good cook so I was well fed.

There were two farms adjoining one another – Stumblehole and Dean. Peggy was in charge of the dairy herd at Dean. One of her two brothers ran the big piggery of pedigree Tamworths and the other was the estate handyman. They were both married with families. Peggy had a smart boyfriend called Robert, who came to see her at weekends.

Nearly all of the people employed on the estate lived in tied cottages. It was like a little village community which revolved around the big Manor House. Everyone knew each other and gossiping was a much practised pastime.

I worked very hard and was allowed half a day off a week, with an extra day off once a month. The first month was unpaid as I was learning how to hand milk the cows, feed the calves, muck out and clean the dairy utensils as well as how to carry two large buckets full of water without slopping it down inside my wellington boots, otherwise I would have to spend the rest of the day with very cold and wet feet. Once I had completed the first month I earned the sum of £2.10 shillings a week.

We had a couple of Italian ex-prisoners of war working on the estate. I became well versed in Italian swear words and familiar with the earthy behaviour of all the farm animals, which proved a far cry from my Nature Study lessons about the birds and the bees. Peggy and her sister-in-law completed many more aspects of my adult education. We all enjoyed working together, jovial banter livened up the days.

We had two Jersey bulls that, although a small breed, are very unpredictable and need to be handled with respect. The cows too could be temperamental, especially when they had just calved. Some were easier to milk than others – there were one or two who would regularly put a foot in the bucket of milk just as I was finishing off milking out the last few drops.

The calves were bucket fed four times a day, so milk was saved for them in churn lids neatly stacked individually on top of the sterilising tank in the dairy. Hidden from the boss's prying eyes at the bottom of the stack were two lids full of rich cream that had craftily been skimmed off from the churns. Peggy used to make this into butter, which at that time was still rationed. It was my job on my half day off to take it to a butcher's shop in Reigate, where it was sold on the black market. For this deadly deed, my perk was a pot of some delicious, freshly churned butter for my family.

I was quite happy joining in the estate happenings; farming folk had a very different type of family life. Every day after lunch we had what was known as our forty winks snooze, to complete the allotted hour. Whoever sat on the sofa had to be careful not to sit on Jane, a miniature dachshund who used to burrow beneath a blanket and was very aggressive if you invaded her personal space.

There were also two well behaved Norwich terriers and Ben, an amorous collie dog, who was fond of the highly bred, pedigree elkhound bitch from the Manor House. Ben was in disgrace when she produced a litter of crossbred puppies, all with four white feet and white tipped tails identical to his.

One of the estate tractor drivers had a pet jackdaw which he had taught to speak like a parrot. Its name was Jacky and she would mimic us when we called the cows in for milking.

All was going well until I succumbed to a deadly type of flu virus which was prevalent that year. I was very ill; the boss's wife was concerned, so she kindly took me home in the Rolls Royce. Unfortunately, I was too ill to enjoy the honour of such a luxurious journey.

It was some time before I fully recovered. Later that year a job came up closer to home looking after some Guernsey house cows and a few pigs and chickens. I applied and was taken on with, I hasten to add, a substantial pay rise. The farm was on Wray Common in Reigate and was complete with a spectacular windmill; it was known as Wray Mill Farm, and owned by a kindly gentleman who was also a Justice of the Peace. His wife had once been his secretary- she was exceedingly fond of a tipple of gin. They had two rather gregarious sons in their twenties. I held the keys to the wonderful old windmill which was no longer in working order, but was just used for storage.

It took about fifteen minutes to cycle to work, and my grandmother only lived five minutes away, so I often called in to see her when I had finished work. I had lunch with the tractor driver and his wife who were very friendly. There were a couple of other men who mostly worked in the garden. The animals were my domain and quite a responsibility at the age of sixteen, although the head gardener did keep a watchful eye on me.

It was fun working there. The cows were all reasonably behaved and easy to manage. Every day I had to go down to the big house to collect the leftover food from the kitchen for the pigs and chickens. I became friendly with the parlour maid and the cook, both of whom were single mothers with their offspring at foot. If the coast was clear they would give me a cup of tea. During Lent they gave up eating cream cakes, which meant I then did very well and so did the pigs!

It was my job to take the milk down to the big house to separate the milk from the cream. The separator resembled a big mincing machine with lots of discs, which had to be assembled in the correct order. The milk was poured into a bowl on top and I had to turn the handle steadily until all had filtered through. Cream came out of one spout and skimmed milk from the other. It was a nightmare to put together and clean afterwards.

On numerous occasions while I was in the dairy I would hear a strange shuffling sound coming along the passage and there, looming in the doorway, would be the rather rotund mistress of the house, lurching forward having to make two or three attempts to get through the door into the dairy. Once in, she would always criticise with a slurred, incoherent volley of words. It was quite a joke to the staff who coped with her very well.

The head gardener smoked a pipe. The tobacco had an interesting aroma and it used to permeate the large potting shed. One day he persuaded me to try, so I copied the way he puffed and almost passed out, it was so strong. He did me a favour – it put me off smoking for life and I never tried again.

On Sunday mornings the boss used to come out when I was milking, to see if I was ok, as everyone else was off duty. He still had his pyjamas on under his trousers; they used to peep out in a little frill around his shoes, which I always found amusing. One day I was giving the little cowshed a spring clean and squirted the walls with water before giving them a scrub. I accidentally sprayed the electric clock on the wall, and as a large part of the wall became live, I was lucky not to have been fatally electrocuted. It certainly gave me one almighty shock!

With my higher wage I could afford the odd riding lesson, and a few weeks later, Biddy, who owned the stables, offered me a job with the ponies. I had always had a passion for horses, so I was happy to grab the opportunity. I soon learnt how to handle each individual character and began to teach the children what to do. It was heels down, hands down and elbows in.

Some of the ponies were out grazing in fields a few miles away so I had to ride a fiery young pony called Champagne, while leading two others, one either side. All went well until on one occasion I encountered road works, complete with a steam roller. Fortunately, the workmen were very helpful. They led the two un-mounted ponies past the steam engine, giving it a very wide berth, while I managed to coax Champagne past, with great difficulty. I sometimes took the ponies to the blacksmith leading them through the middle of Reigate, which was not so busy in those days, but would be impossible with all the traffic that passes through the town today.

By the time they had been caught and ridden back to the stables from the field, they were usually quiet enough for the children to ride. Some of the ponies were great characters. One little pony called Sooty used to do her utmost to tread on the toes of whoever was leading her, and Charlie had a tendency to try to roll if he did not like whoever was in the saddle. Matilda kicked and Henry never wanted to be caught. At times it was a nightmare keeping everything running smoothly and I just trusted to luck that every one returned home unscathed.

I had quite a number of young helpers who were pony mad; they worked a few hours to earn free rides. Sometimes I had to exercise ponies out over Earlswood Common to burn off their excess energy before they had children on board. Whiz was a large cob who was full of mischief; he would spook at the slightest opportunity and one day he bolted, with me on his back, right out on to the main road. Fortunately, there was not too much traffic that day.

The vet who had attended to the animals at both of my previous jobs also turned up at the stables. I soon realised that he was keen on Biddy. He was Irish and his name was David. He had a great sense of humour, and told many amusing tales. He would find any excuse to call in at the stables. One evening he took Biddy to Tex Ritter's Wild West show in London. Later that year when the show finished, David bought two of the horses who had performed in it. One was The Mighty Atom, a wild and wicked bucking bronco and the other a quiet, rather under-nourished mare that had been the mount of a glamorous lady who sang in four octaves. It was my job to look after them. The Mighty Atom was a real handful. I had to take him for a walk every day in Reigate Priory, during which time he thought he was still performing.

David was intrigued as to why he behaved in such an unpredictable manner, so he gave him an anesthetic and on closer examination discovered that his testicles had been cruelly tampered with, which had somewhat confused his testosterone levels. While the horse was still under the anesthetic, David gelded him properly and as the weeks went by The Mighty Atom slowly became a more manageable animal.

I had thought I would like to study at agricultural college, but as my mother was inclined to think that further education was wasted on girls, I had to do the next best thing and continued to gain hands on experience at different types of agriculturally linked employment. The benefit of choosing that way forward was that I earned wages, so it wasn't such a bad idea. Therefore my next job was with a small Guernsey herd along with a few pigs and chickens at Lowbridge Farm, Leigh, near Reigate.

I was then seventeen and my father had bought me a second hand auto-cycle which was like a small motor bike. I passed my driving test so was able to commute to and from work in style. There were just three of us working on the farm. I looked after the animals and Dick was the tractor driver. He shared the general maintenance with a friendly man from Lithuania who, like so many, had stayed on after the war. We worked well together and Dick, who had a wicked sense of humour, kept us amused. He used to hard boil eggs for us in the dairy kettle. On one occasion he dared me to swallow a raw egg whole, which I managed to do with great difficulty while they goaded me on.

The chickens were kept in large arks which were fully enclosed with a small house and nest box at one end and a large run under wire netting at the other. They were fox and vermin proof and were moved daily onto fresh grass to allow the hens to scratch about happily. The Lithuanian used to call it moving the chicken village. It was an excellent way to keep laying hens until the winter weather turned freezing. Then trying to thaw and re-fill the water feeders became a thankless task.

I had a very narrow squeak with Mini, one of the newly calved cows. I was putting iodine on the calf's navel to stop any infection, when Mini, being overly calf proud, rammed me against the wall of the loose box. Fortunately Dick came to my rescue and I emerged somewhat bruised but extremely grateful that he was working nearby and had come in time to stop what could have been a very nasty incident.

I used to look forward to the delivery of cattle food as the driver was a handsome young man with a wicked twinkle in his eye. He always used to tease me and comment on my check shirts. As the years slowly rolled by, we bumped into one another from time to time and the smile and twinkle were still there. He worked for the same firm until he retired.

It was around this time that my parents were planning to visit my father's relations in Switzerland. I asked my employers if it would be possible to have my holiday at the same time so I could go too. They refused, so I left their employment and visited Glion, my grandmother's home way up in the mountains above Montreux, where we met many relations. It was so interesting, observing various family traits in cousins who we had never met before. It was a welcome break from the hard grind of work.

I was still visiting Biddy's riding stables at odd times and one of her many friends was manager of a dairy farm near Merstham. It was near enough for me to reach on my auto cycle, so I accepted a job there to work with Jersey cows again. There I met Dot, who remained a life long friend and Wally who was an ex-Polish soldier who also had stayed on after the war. Wally owned a motor bike and had a working collie dog who would sit up on the tank in front of him while he drove at breakneck speed.

Shortly after I started at Oakley Farm, the manager left, taking a job abroad. A new younger man took over straight from university. He was very full of his own importance and was not sure how to handle a couple of eighteen year old girls, who gave him rather a hard time! He lived in a cottage that went with his job. He asked us one day to light a type of wood burner for him as he was not very domesticated. Dot managed to get it going, but in the process nearly blew the stove up when she threw paraffin on just to give it a little encouragement. While we were in the house we turned all his saucy pin-ups upside down. He was not amused.

Dot had a little motor bike too, so we were both quite mobile. We joined the Merstham Old Time Dance Club. It was great fun and one evening at dusk when the dancing had finished, we thought it would be fun to see how brave the arrogant young manager was. Just outside his cottage garden was a field of tall maize, which was almost ready for harvesting. We made odd noises by the house then hid in the maize. We watched with amusement when he came out, but then to our dismay we realised he was carrying a shotgun. We had to lie low until he went back in and closed the door, and when we judged the timing to be safe, scurried back to our motorbikes and made our escape. He was difficult to work for in many ways and we could see that our days there were probably numbered. Dot and I decided it was definitely time to move on.

CHAPTER 7

Priory Mead Veterinary Surgery

I was lucky enough to be invited to the rather lively parties David and Biddy used to throw, and for the first time I saw how the other half lived. They had both been married and divorced, and David was now ready to set up a new veterinary surgery at the large house he bought, complete with stables, situated between Reigate town and The Priory. It was called Priory Mead. During one of these parties, David proposed to Biddy while playing "sardines" under a bed, sardines being a game where one person hides and each person who discovers the hiding place has to cram into the same place, hence packed like sardines. I happened to be the first to learn the news, and then the celebrations began in earnest, as one by one we all ended up under the bed. On a previous occasion canoodling had taken place in the larder and the ration books had accidentally been knocked into the egg preserving pail. The preservative had totally obliterated the indelible ink on some of the coupons, so we were able to have extra rations.

Shortly after the engagement they were married and David and Biddy set up home together, at Priory Mead. Biddy acquired her pet horse Whiz, for hunting. He had been sold as unrideable but Biddy loved a challenge as nobody had ridden him without being thrown off. He was a perfect gentleman to handle in the stable, but it was a different story once he was being ridden. He bucked me off twenty two times in all, giving me quite a few cracks and bruises.

Whiz was turned out in a large field to graze with other horses for the summer months. One Sunday afternoon I went with David and Biddy to check that they were ok. Biddy could not resist giving Whiz a little exercise and rode him round the field bare-back. It was a crazy decision.

All went well until one of the other horses cut in front. Whiz shied to one side to avoid it and Biddy came off, falling heavily on her leg and was trampled on by the other horses. David and I rushed over to find she had serious compound fractures, with bones sticking right through the skin on her leg. David immediately whisked her off to hospital. It was up to me to sort out the horses and the other animals back at the surgery. Indeed, it was a very traumatic time, not knowing just how bad Biddy's injuries were.

I left my job at Merstham to hold the fort for David at the surgery. Biddy was battered and badly bruised but slowly recovered from her injuries. She came home from hospital a few weeks later with her leg in plaster. There was never a dull moment. I helped with the everyday chores which included being a veterinary nurse – sterilising and preparing all the instruments and assisting David with operations on small animals, scrubbing up before and afterwards and remaining on watch as the animals came round from their anaesthetic.

Sometimes we had to go out at unearthly hours to help with difficult calving cases. There were also the cats and dogs who were boarding that had to be cared for too. In between times I went shopping for our groceries as Reigate town was just round the corner, I tidied up the garden and sometimes delivered medicines to local folk who did not have transport. Mrs Dicky came in on weekdays to cook and clean, and on her days off I would perform her duties in the house too. Biddy always came first. I helped her to bath without getting her plaster wet and made sure she was comfortable and had everything she needed to keep her happy and occupied until she was fully recovered.

Whiz, Biddy's beloved horse, and a young mare were in the stables beside the house. I used to exercise him to keep him fit, ready for hunting. One day I was riding him out over Reigate Heath when he was startled by a large dog emerging from the undergrowth. Whiz gave a massive leap to one side then jumped back to front, dropped me, and headed across the heath for home. I picked myself up, my heart pounding, praying that he would not career across the main road. Bruised and stumbling I staggered over the rough ground after him. On the way I met an old man who said, "Av you lost your 'orse? 'Ee went that er way!" pointing in the direction of home. Whiz had actually taken himself home to his stable. Fortunately he had arrived none the worse for wear, which is more than I could say for myself. I eventually made it back on foot, half an hour after Whiz, who I swear grinned at the sight of me, covered in mud as he happily munched away at his hay.

I found helping David with the operations fascinating. They were very varied and on one occasion, a dog came in whose owner thought it had swallowed her wedding ring. David opened it up and carefully searched, feeling through the whole of its intestines only to find a key for opening a sardine tin. Alas, there was no wedding ring. Luckily, the dog made a complete recovery.

Another day, as the clock struck eleven, the doorbell of the veterinary surgery chimed, heralding the next appointment. Silhouetted through the glass panelled door I opened the door to a huge man with a large dog at heel.

"Good morning Mr. Buckle, come in, so you've brought Bruno in to have his dewclaws removed. It's just a minor operation and shouldn't take long. Would you like to stay and watch?"

"Yes, if I may," he replied, giving a slightly nervous smile.

"Bring him through," I said, holding the door open into the operating theatre.

Bruno, a large Alsatian dog, was not impressed. As we lifted him up onto the operating table, we were greeted with a deep throated growl and a quivering top lip, which curled upwards displaying a fine set of glistening white teeth, ready for action. Without hesitation I managed to wind a bandage tightly round his nose before they inflicted any damage.

David eyed him suspiciously. "As he tends to be aggressive, I think a general anaesthetic is the best option," he said, reaching for a syringe.

As I glanced at Mr Buckle, I noticed droplets of perspiration beginning to trickle down the burly man's forehead. "Are you ok watching this, Mr. Buckle?" I asked, squeezing a vein on Bruno's leg ready for the needle.

"Yes, I'm fine, I did Army training as a lad and we did first aid then," he said, trying to calm Bruno down.

David inserted the needle and Bruno slowly sank down and was strapped to the operating table. While I cleaned the dewclaws with spirit, David selected a large scalpel from the sterilizer. I held the first dewclaw in forceps and David sliced into the skin. When blood spurted out, Mr.

Buckle's ruddy complexion gradually turned from very pale to ghastly white. Before he passed out, I enquired, "Would you like to go and sit in the waiting room?"

"Y-yes p-please," he stammered. I escorted him out. His legs gave way as he collapsed into a chair. "Oh, thank you, I feel such a twit," he whispered.

"Don't worry, it's not the first time it's happened," I assured him. They both made a full recovery. He was definitely not the only person who reacted in that way, and it seemed surprising to me that it was always the people you least expected who struggled with the sight of blood.

One night the telephone rang just as I was about to go to bed. It was a farmer who had a cow having difficulty calving. I went with David, who after a struggle, managed to deliver a very large, dead bull calf. Little did I know, as I helped George the farmer, drag the corpse into a hovel away from the cow, that one day in the not too distant future, he was to figure largely in my life.

On a sunny afternoon when I was doing a spot of gardening behind the stables, a dog came in that had been run over. It appeared to be as dead as a doornail on arrival. David was out on a mission so Biddy checked to make sure it was dead then I helped her put it in a special bin for the collection of dead animals. I resumed my weeding. A few minutes later the bin lid started to move. I realized that the unfortunate, badly injured animal was showing signs of life. Biddy and I lifted him out of the bin and Biddy gave him a final injection through the heart to end his pain, and thankfully afterwards the bin lid remained tightly closed.

I had to hold the bigger dogs when they had to be put down. They were usually shot with a humane killer while they were happily sniffing around the dung heap and knew nothing of their fate.

For a little light relief, Jack O'Donaghue, whose stables were just down the road at the entrance to Reigate Priory, used to come in for supper and to bathe sometimes. He lived for a while in a converted loose box beside his horses. Like David, he was Irish and would keep us amused with all his interesting horse stories. One that remains in my memory is about a horse named Western Slipper who had simply been pulling a milk float, delivering milk in Ireland, before he went into training and became a famous racehorse. Jack later became a successful racehorse trainer, renowned for training difficult horses. He trained Nickel Coin for the Queen Mother and caused much excitement when it won the Grand National for her, back in the 1950s, beating a horse named Royal Tan. They were the only two left in the race at the finish. I remember how exciting it was watching the race unfold on television.

Tricksy and Liz were two rescued dogs. Tricksy, a Jack Russell, had been brought in and was waiting to be put down but she boldly walked through as though she owned the place, jumped up on David's bed and snuggled down for the night, which won everybody over and gave her a reprieve.

Biddy had found Liz, a Labrador cross, abandoned and took her in. I was fond of them; they became a much loved part of the household. Last thing at night I would run them down to the Priory gates and back to spend their last pennies before bed. One night as I was about to walk past the waiting room, which was by the front door, a white apparition appeared. My heart started racing and I felt my blood pressure rise, before I realised that it was David, covered in a white sheet, playing one of his jokes. It took me a day or two to forgive him.

Another night when I returned from a Young Farmers' meeting, the house was in darkness, so I thought everyone was having an early night. I was quietly opening the door and about to creep in when there was one almighty crash. I almost jumped out of my skin. The dogs went berserk and then all the lights came on. David, Biddy and friends who were visiting enjoyed the joke, having ingeniously rigged up the booby trap ready for my entrance. I soon recovered from the shock and was welcomed in to join the party.

Minnie, Biddy's ginger cat used to jump up on the table which was not allowed, so one day David whisked her off and pretended she was a set of bagpipes. He put her tail to his mouth, tucked her head under his arm then squeezed her until she let out an enormous yowl, which sounded just like an Irish Bagpipe starting up. She never jumped on the table again.

Tricksy was mated to an intelligent little hunt terrier and nine weeks later she produced a litter of cute puppies. I fell in love with one in particular and when they were old enough to leave their mother, Biddy offered one to me. Sadly my Mother would not let me have her in the house. I waited a few days and thought that if she saw it, she might change her mind. I took the puppy home and was heartbroken when Mother told me that I could just take it back where it had come from. With hindsight, it was probably for the best, as although I thought I could train it to sit in my auto-cycle pannier, not everybody allows their staff to bring dogs to work.

I think that the reason behind this rejection was the fact it brought back painful memories for my Mother. She had owned a dog called Jack; he was a wire haired terrier that my grandfather had rescued after the dog was in trouble for killing a neighbour's chickens. He gave it to Mother to guard and keep her company while my Father was on night duty, in the police force. All went well until Jack took a dislike to my Dad. I think that the feeling was mutual. However, Jack took to running back to my Grandfather's home. One day my mother came home to find that sadly, Jack was dead. It later transpired that my dad had gassed him!

While I was still working at David and Biddy's I decided to have my ears pierced. David offered to pierce them for me, so I bought some sleepers, which are earrings for newly pierced ears. I was advised to boil up the earrings along with the curved needle with a cutting blade that was used to stitch up the wounds of small animals. Everything was in order, complete with white spirit to clean off my ear lobes. Biddy and a friend called Wallace Smedley, quite famous at the time for Smedley's tinned peas, stood by to watch.

I sat down and leaned over so that my ear lobe rested on the table while David made the hole with the needle which wiggled a little when it went through. The second piercing benefitted from the experience gained after David's first try, and the needle went straight through with no trouble. The next challenge was to put the sleepers in, and as my ears were bleeding profusely, it was a messy job. However, Wallace volunteered and managed to thread them through. Fortunately, there is not a lot of feeling in ear lobes, it's just gristle. The next morning I looked in the mirror at my two bruised ears but was pleased with my new attachments until I discovered that one was slightly crooked and stuck out sideways. David offered to repeat the process at a later date but I declined, and to this day one still has a slight list to starboard.

Biddy changed her mind about letting David pierce her ears. She decided to go to a jeweller as they used a special instrument. I've been told it can also be done with a red hot needle and a cork.

I had enjoyed my time at the surgery and had gained much valuable experience but yearned for the outdoor life again. I knew that I could always pop in to see them on my days off, and Biddy and David remained lifelong friends.

David suggested that I take a trip to his home in Ireland before I started a new job and while I had the opportunity. He arranged for me to stay with his relations, so we booked a flight.

I was excited at the thought of flying for the first time but also slightly apprehensive, not knowing what to expect. I was quite relieved when we landed at Nutts Corner Airfield, Belfast. I felt as though I had been sealed in a tube.

David's eldest sister met me and as we passed through Belfast on the way to her home I was surprised to see a couple of men asleep on the pavement, I presumed 'Brahms and Liszt' as the result of an overload of Guiness.

I enjoyed the next few days sightseeing and a stay with David's younger sister, who lived on a farm with her husband and two teenage sons. She taught me how to make soda bread.

The countryside was beautiful but the way things were done seemed many years behind the times. I was intrigued by a wooden gadget that was fitted into the stream running past the house. As it filled up, the weight of the water tipped it, which made it work like a pump to supply water to the buildings.

One afternoon when I helped to hand milk the cows an elderly neighbour, who had learning difficulties, found himself a milking stool and sat and grinned at me all the time I was milking. When one started to bat me round the head with her dirty tail he sat behind her and held it still. It was quite touching; he treated me as if I was royalty.

I was interested to discover how the Irish grew potatoes. I spent a day helping one of the sons cut seed potatoes into three. Most potatoes are shaped a little like a heart, so we had to cut the bottom part off for the pigs and then the top, from where the shoots grew, was cut into two, thus doubling the crop and it helped feed the pigs too.

The two weeks went quickly and it was soon time to be re-incarcerated in a plane to fly back home, ready to start my new job.

CHAPTER 8

Odd Jobs, Helping Out ... and Fate

Once Biddy was up on her feet again and able to cope, I went to work for the Jupps family. They were David and Biddy's party friends and were desperate for help with their two young children and animals. They had recently acquired a smallholding beside Redhill common. I went to give them a hand, just until they found a suitable nanny and handyman.

The Mighty Atom, the pony David had rescued from The Tex Ritters Show in London, was given a home with the Jupps while waiting for his gelding to take full effect. It was already several months since his operation but he still behaved like a lunatic, bucking, kicking and squealing as he dive-bombed anyone approaching him in the field.

Once the Jupps had settled in and had found permanent staff, I thought it was a golden opportunity to take a holiday, especially as one of my Scottish cousins was getting married and the whole of that side of the family would be meeting in St. Andrew's for the occasion. I travelled up alone and stayed with relations. It was fun to be back with all the cousins that I had been to school with during our wartime evacuation.

We met many times in the two weeks that I was there. One of the most memorable was when we decided to hire some horses to ride across the West Sands while the tide was out. I remember I rode a horse called Rob-Roy. It was exhilarating galloping over the Sands, with the wind blowing through my hair all the way to the river Eden, then letting him paddle in the sea to cool off on the journey back home to his stable.

One evening we all decided to go to a dance. My cousin Albert had promised to see me safely home when it had finished. The original family home where I was staying with two maiden aunts was a large flat above a shop selling all dairy produce, situated in the main street. The dance finished at midnight, but by that time Albert had found a rather voluptuous blonde who also needed escorting home. Knowing that one of his friends was keen to walk me back, we said goodnight and went our separate ways. All was fine until we arrived at the shop doorway when my escort became vastly more amorous than I had bargained for. There were quite a few empty milk bottles left in the corner by the door and in the ensuing embrace they were knocked over and with one almighty clatter they rolled down over the pavement into the gutter. My newfound lover retreated as lights from neighbouring flats came on to investigate the cause of the noise at such an unearthly hour. I crept in, once all was quiet and the lights had gone out, hoping that my aunts were blissfully sleeping at the back of the flat, unaware of the commotion.

As it happened, my cousin's wedding was called off, but I had a wonderful holiday nonetheless.

It was around this time that my sister and brother-in-law, who had a pig farm, were planning a well earned holiday and were looking for someone to look after the pigs. I volunteered and went to help a few weeks before the holiday was due, so I could become fully conversant with the feeding routine. There were pigs of all sizes everywhere. The babies were in a huge indoor house, and then as they grew they were transferred into sties outside according to their various age groups, and were fed accordingly.

Their diet consisted of swill; leftover food which, by Ministry Regulations, had to be cooked in order to kill any bugs that could cause infections or viruses, such as Foot and Mouth Disease. In order to comply with the rules, my brother-in-law Harry, had devised an ingenious method. A drum full of old oil was slowly dripped down a chute on to a flame; this heated a huge cauldron full of swill suspended above the fire. Fortunately there were no neighbours living nearby because it gave off a mighty stench that permeated the early morning mist across the top of Reigate Hill. However the pigs found it appetising, especially when it was mixed with stale bread and cakes which boosted their carbohydrate levels. These were collected from many London bakeries by a huge old removal lorry. It was quite exciting to find that much of it was hardly stale and some of the cakes were edible and delicious.

In the meantime, David the vet had been rushed into hospital with a haemorrhaging stomach ulcer. Moving house and surgery and generally sorting out his life over the previous few years had taken its toll on his health, so I went back to stay with Biddy. A locum had to be found to keep the practice going. A vet from New Zealand came but didn't stay very long. He was a strange guy and I did not feel comfortable working with him. He gave me the creeps. I was helping him one evening while Biddy had gone to visit David in hospital. After the surgery had finished there was a dog to be put down but instead of giving it one injection to put it to sleep, he only gave it a slight amount, then experimented with all sorts of different drugs to watch the reaction to see how it responded, before he administered the final dose. I was completely horrified by his actions, and told Biddy. His days were numbered and a retired vet and his wife from Yorkshire came to take his place.

Sometimes I went with Biddy to visit David in hospital, and as he was on the mend he was moved further up the ward away from the door. He still retained his sense of humour, as he had been noticing that the sicker the patients became the nearer to the door they were moved, ready for their demise. David would report gruesome daily details as to whether any, or how many, 'stiffies' had departed from the ward that day.

When David came out of hospital, Biddy and he went for a holiday and I stayed on with the Yorkshire couple. They were both charming; she taught me how to make proper Yorkshire pudding. They remained at Priory Mead until David had fully recovered.

I was thrilled when David and Biddy invited me to an evening out at a variety show at the Brighton Hippodrome. It was one of their favourite haunts and somewhere that I had never been before. It was a new experience for me, and a most enjoyable thank you present.

Once everything was back to normal and running smoothly I was keen to return to farming, as I much preferred to be out in the fresh air. David knew many farmers. At first I was going to work on a large estate, where they knew the manager, Charles Nye, but it was miles away in Hampshire. It was then decided that there would be a vacancy on the farm that Charles Nye actually owned and that his son was managing. It was much nearer to my home near Reigate. It turned out to be none other than George Nye, the farmer who had called David out late at night to help him with a cow called Nannette, who had given birth to a dead breeched calf. I didn't know it then, but fate had shown her hand and my hardworking but carefree life was about to change forever, as on Valentines Day in 1952 I started working for George Nye at Kinnersley Manor Farm near Reigate.

I was eighteen years old and was happy to be working with a herd of Ayrshire cows. They had a more placid temperament than the Channel Island cattle I had worked with before. I was keen to learn about the importance of good grassland management for milk production. As a youngster I had thought that grass was just grass, but at The Young Farmers' Meetings I learned that wasn't the case and I discovered there is much more to farming. It is the science of nature and there are very many different varieties of grass which all contain vastly different nutrients depending on the type of soil they are grown on. There is the permanent pasture, grass that has been down for years and natural to its surroundings but often not so productive. This is fine for horses and sheep but to produce more milk, research discovered that by blending certain grasses together they can be successfully grown for four or five years until the wild grasses take over again. Once this has happened they are ploughed up and corn (or some other crop) is grown there for a year. The ground is Ph tested after the harvest, then carefully blended grass mixtures best suited to the local terrain are sown again, they are known as four or five year leys. George had won trophies for his skilled grassland management.

I settled into my new job well and enjoyed working with Colin, the other student, and Sid, the cowman who lived with his wife and family in a tied cottage on the farm, owned by George's father. What had once been a large estate had been split many ways. The Manor House had been turned into flats and the cottages had been sold off separately. George had built a smart new bungalow for himself, his wife Louise and their two little girls.

Early one morning, soon after I started working there, I arrived to find that there had been great excitement. George had caught a burglar and wrestled him to the ground. When he called for help, people in the flats looked out and saw George waving a stick while he stood over a man, but thought that it was just a brawl. Finally they realised what was happening and called the Police, who came to his aid. It made the headlines of the weekly newspaper, which read: "Local Farmer's Early Morning Chase." George was highly commended and the much wanted burglar went to jail. George remained calm and unassuming and handled it as though it had been an every day event.

The routine at Kinnersley was much the same as I had been used to, except that the milking machines were different and the milk was still collected in churns. One day I was rolling a churn full of milk from the dairy, ready for collection, when the lid came off and almost all the ten gallons gurgled down the dairy drain just as George put his head around the dairy door. I thought he would sack me on the spot, but to my relief he just grinned and said that he didn't think I would do it again in a hurry!'

Sometimes I used to babysit the little girls so that their parents could have an evening out. Before I went to work for George, Biddy had warned me that there was a 'rift in the loot', meaning that all was not well with the marriage. Biddy and David had socialised with George and Louise and Biddy could see that things were not quite as they should be between them. It wasn't until I was sent to put fertiliser on the fields that were furthest from the farm buildings that my own suspicions were aroused. George would arrive to see how I was getting on. I must admit I did find that lifting hundred weight bags of fertiliser up into the spreader was back breaking so I always appreciated a hand, but driving round the fields on the tractor scattering it out was enjoyable, especially on a beautiful spring day. On one occasion George came and filled up the hopper of the spreader for me and stopped for a chat. As he was leaving he gave me a little paper bag and said that it was something to keep me going. Before I started work again, I opened the bag and found a bar of chocolate. I decided to treat myself to a piece there and then. What a surprise I got as I started to undo the wrapper and there, tucked neatly underneath the paper I found a Durex condom. I was so shocked, and wondered what sort of girl George thought I was. I remembered then Biddy's warning. Ten out of ten for originality George, but I was not going to accept his "invitation"! The most embarrassing part for me was I had to go back at milking time and I knew I had to deal with him face to face. I decided that the only thing I could do was to ignore the whole matter and pretend I hadn't noticed the extra "gift". It was so disappointing because I was happy in my work and it was so convenient – just fifteen minutes from home on my auto cycle. Things would never be the same again.

One day that summer, at haymaking time I spent the whole day standing in the middle of a field in a sweltering heat wave, threading wires through a stationary baler. The next day I was too ill to go to work, suffering from a terrible dose of sunstroke which lasted several days. George came to see how I was, which surprised my suspicious father who realised there was more to this innocent visit than met the eye. That evening he told me I had to leave my job, or he said he would make me a ward of court. I was nineteen and I really don't think he could have carried out his threat, but I was in a difficult situation and decided it would be better if I did leave Kinnersley Manor and the attentions of George.

It was not long before I found another job, and in the autumn of 1952 I started working with a large herd of pedigree Friesian cows at Runtley Wood Farm, Sutton Green, near Guildford. It was a beautiful spot with a canal which linked up with the River Wey, running along the boundary at Send, where there was a lock gate and a picturesque lock keeper's cottage.

I lived in a little shack beside the farm manager's house and ate my meals with the cowman, his wife and their little boy. The food was not too good; the cows had a more balanced diet than we did. Fortunately, the little boy was very finicky so I used to finish up all the food he left and I drank a considerable amount of milk at milking time to compensate. On Christmas day I offered to do all the milking to give the cowman a day off. A small bowl of stewed chicken giblets was left for my meal for the day – not much of a reward for my well intended gesture! The shack was very primitive; it was really just a shed but I had a bed, a dressing table, a chair, an electric fire and a radio. The wages were good and I had one day off a week.

The cows were milked three times a day so we worked shifts. One day we milked very early in the morning, midday and late evening. The next day we spent doing various chores – mucking out, preparing all the food and washing down. That system meant we were able to have half the afternoon and the whole evening off, which worked very well, enabling me to go into Guildford or Woking without having to rush back. It was a prize herd and every drop of milk from each cow was recorded. One dear old cow called Runtley Wood Diana had won an award for producing over 100 tons of milk. She no longer had a sylph- like figure but was still producing a calf annually.

It was freezing cold travelling on my auto cycle in the middle of winter. I used to leave home on a Sunday evening just as Victor Sylvester's signature tune came on the radio. It used to take me about an hour to return to the shack. Then one horrible, freezing, dark night George's van loomed up out of the fog and he offered to put my auto cycle in the back and give me a lift to the farm. Under the circumstances I found it difficult to refuse, so I gratefully accepted the offer. Inevitably this became a regular occurrence and I will always remember how beautifully the nightingales sang at the top of Newlands Corner the following spring!

The arrangement and meetings with George was working well, until one evening my father arrived unannounced at my shack in a furious rage. He had discovered that I was still seeing George, and as I was not yet twenty one my father was adamant that I was still under his control. With language angry enough to turn the air blue, my father ordered me to leave my job. I decided that to prevent bloodshed I would comply!

CHAPTER 9

Working in Veterinary Research

I found an interesting job in veterinary research in East Sussex. The company was based in a huge mansion house surrounded by a large estate which consisted of four farms. On the main farm was a herd of milking cows, another one had stables where the two resident stallions stood, along with a few mares that were privately owned.

There was another big compound where dogs were housed. Vaccines for Distemper and other diseases were being developed at that time. Where I worked animals were being observed and monitored for a variety of research projects. I should stress that the animals were treated humanely, and I never witnessed any animal being treated with anything but respect.

The girls I worked with were all very fond of animals. We lived in the servant quarters on the top floor of the house. The second floor was where visiting vets and guests stayed. If there were no visitors we used to sneak down for a luxury bath because the bathrooms were very posh, with mirrors and highly polished tiles, much better than ours.

We had a rota for cooking and those on duty who were first down to the kitchen in the morning had to lift several upturned pots and dispose of the cockroaches that had been trapped overnight, before we proceeded to cook the breakfast. It was common practice for us to hang our washing out to dry on a line in a concealed part of the roof when nobody was around, often at midnight.

It was fun to be with single girls of my age. Ruth had a passion for collecting caterpillars and one night some escaped. We found them in the morning working their way down the banisters to the ground floor below.

It took ages rounding them all up. Anne had a collection of tiny bottled foetuses floating in preserving fluid, adorning the shelf in her room.

Most of us belonged to the local Young Farmers' Club and we went on some interesting trips. One of the most memorable was a supper party in an oast house, when beer making was in progress. It was at the time when Londoners came down with the whole family for a holiday, to pick the hops. They were a jolly crowd and finished the evening singing Cockney songs.

I found my work very interesting, caring for animals being observed for hormone research and also monitoring the cycle of various worms, especially lung worms.

There were a dozen big strong mares of mixed breeding. We were allocated three each to look after. I was in charge of Tiny, a huge mare who was over seventeen hands high; Schnapps, a mare with a voracious appetite for human flesh and a friendly mare called Beth, both around the sixteen hands mark. The mares were covered by one or other of the resident stallions who were old and experienced but past working for their original stud.

It was not until later that I realised how famous they were. One was Fairway, whose genes still circulate in the blood of most thoroughbred horses today and the other was from the famous Black Stephan line. Both had been donated to the company to end their days in a leisurely fashion, just covering our mares and the private thoroughbred racing mares that were having problems getting in foal.

On Sundays the stallion man, who was also the shepherd, had his day off, so the girls had to take it in turns to feed them. The stallions were both very cheeky and would challenge us by rearing up and striking out with their front feet, just trying to ascertain who was boss as we went in to feed them. I tried to appear calm and relaxed, but it is amazing how horses, especially stallions, instantly pick up human vibes.

A cow called Princess was another of my specialities; she was barren when she came in from the herd. Every morning, I had to listen to her heartbeat through a stethoscope and carefully record its rate, along with her respiration and her general behaviour. She was having hormone injections and it wasn't long before Princess began to behave like a Prince, pawing at the ground and bellowing like a bull.

I also had to look after a dozen young heifers from the herd that were suffering from a type of cough known as husk, which was caused by lung worms. It was my job to collect a sample of faeces from each one and listen and record the duration and density of their coughing. On occasions, when I couldn't identify the owner of the faeces and it was knocking off time, I had to put my hand in and help myself to a sample before I could go off duty.

The journey around the body of mammals by many different types of worms was truly amazing and was carefully monitored. They were trying to develop wormers to reduce the devastating effect that many of these parasites caused, both to animals and human beings.

We had other small animals to work with, such as rabbits, hedgehogs, coypu and tropical rats. We were not allowed to know too much about what was going on, just in case we were spies from another company. There was always a race as to which pharmaceutical firm could develop the first successful treatments. Later, many of the rival firms amalgamated.

Once a week we had to be at work early in the morning to assist with sheep bleeding. A specially selected batch of Wethers, which are castrated rams, were rounded up and lifted onto specially made racks while a measured amount of their blood was taken from the main artery. The bottles contained glass beads and as the blood ran into the bottles we had to shake them hard to stop it from clotting. The blood was then rushed up to London by a van, already waiting, ready to deliver it to a laboratory for human research- the sheep appeared not to mind. There were several batches of them, so they happily went out to graze until it was their turn again, several weeks later.

The main professional staff and laboratories were up at the Mansion. Seminars were arranged for vets who came from all over the world to gain experience on the latest treatments that had been developed. Sometimes we had to walk the mares up to the next farm so the visitors could practise examining them, trying to diagnose which ones were in foal. This was of course long before scanning devices were available.

The visiting vets were given accommodation at the Mansion. There was always a lively farewell party and dance on the final night of the seminars, to which the entire staff was invited. At one of these parties, I was having something of a problem with a gentleman from the Caribbean, who was getting a little carried away, when the boss of the establishment noticed his behaviour. He kindly rescued me by asking me for the next dance. I was relieved and very flattered as I polkaed around the dance floor with him. The boss's spinster sister was always put on duty at the Mansion on ball nights to ensure that no hanky panky went on after the last dance.

Tunbridge Wells was the nearest town and it had a good shopping centre. The Pantiles, the original part where the ancient wells are, was fascinating to walk round on my days off. On the days when I went home I usually found George waiting en route.

I enjoyed my time in veterinary research, although the wages were not too good. I learnt an enormous amount of valuable, interesting information there. Sadly, we heard that the large animals were going to another branch of the company as our branch went on to research and develop vaccines, much of which involved propagating the viruses in fertile eggs. So, the girls from our department who had been caring for the large animals had a farewell party, we said our goodbyes and went our separate ways.

I managed to find a responsible job as head herdswoman, complete with a cottage and good wages, on a Dairy Farm at Withyham, in East Sussex.

CHAPTER 10

Summerford Farm

It was in November 1953, when I was twenty years old, that I started work as head Herdswoman with a show herd of Dairy Shorthorns, under the watchful eyes of the owners, Mr and Mrs Chambers, at Summerford Farm, Withyham in East Sussex. The wages were very good and a tied cottage went with the job. At first I lodged with Mabel and Bill Keeler. They were great characters from bygone days. Bill worked on the farm and Mabel in the farmhouse, and Bill taught me many fascinating, old fashioned ideas and remedies regarding the care of livestock. Mabel had a placid nature and a heart of gold. She smoked heavily and was continually flicking the ash off the end of her cigarette with a finger. Their tied farm cottage was very old; it joined on to the one next door where Edie, her husband Bob and her brother Jack lived. They all worked on the farm. Jack was the carter who looked after the two cart horses; they were his pride and joy. He liked a drink and used to spend his spare time at the local pub, the Dorset Arms. At closing time he would be turned out and faced in the direction of home. He would stagger through the village but despite his condition, he never forgot to rack up his horses with hay as he passed by the stables. Then he would continue on up the one in four steep hill to the cottage, where he slept in a chair downstairs for the night. Jack and his brother-in-law Bob had not spoken to one another for many years. One day, poor Edie, who had seen better days, was rushed to hospital and Mabel went in to the cottage to pack a bag for her with the things she needed, only to find the place in a terrible state. There were even mice nesting in Edie's spare nightdress!

Each cottage had a bucket loo in a little brick building in the garden with a pigsty built on the other end. There was no gas or electricity, just candles and oil lamps. I remember sometimes Bill used to wash the dishes by stacking them all neatly in the sink, then with a large kettle full of boiling water, he would hold it high above the dishes and with a circular motion pour it all over them. It did a pretty good job as there was seldom anything left to scrape off afterwards. In the evenings Bill used to play records on an old wind up gramophone. His favourite was called "Over the Garden Wall", a song with very funny lyrics about all the things that went on over a garden wall, witnessed by a neighbour.

In the night when all was quiet, rats came through from next door; they would scuttle about under the floorboards and made such a clatter it sounded as though they were wearing football boots! One night I was woken up as one ran over me in bed. I was petrified and lay there in the dark for a while, praying it would not make a return journey using the same route. I was so tired that I soon dropped off again. The next day traps were set in the little bedroom next to mine and we caught five. Then there were the fleas. Mabel assured me that if I folded my bed clothes back up when I went out to milk early in the morning, she would have caught the offending livestock by breakfast time. Her theory was that as the bed cooled down, the fleas always crept up into the warmest part under the pillow. Sure enough, she presented me with a couple in a match box coffin at breakfast time.

It was decided, before any of us succumbed to some deadly disease, that Mabel, Bill and I would move into the dairy cottage which went with my job as soon as it became vacant. It was next door to the big farmhouse which stood by the River Medway and conveniently much closer to the farmyard. It was larger, much more modern and easy to clean and came with electricity and a flushing toilet and without rats or fleas!

Food was still rationed at this time but living on a farm there was plenty of milk and eggs. Many people grew their own vegetables. Mabel dished up stewed breast of lamb swimming in greasy gravy most days, but we were grateful nonetheless for a nutritious, hot meal.

The herd of Shorthorn cows was good to work with. The heifer calves were kept for herd replacements and the bull calves were fattened up for meat, so there were effectively two separate herds. The milking was done by machine but after cooling it was still collected in ten gallon churns. I used to take a few pints into the farmhouse for cream. I poured it into a very large bowl, and in the morning the cream had risen to the top. I skimmed it off with a large spatula, carefully spooning it into a second bowl for the cook in the big house, making sure to leave it coated with plenty of thick cream to lick off as my reward, before washing it up. There were pigs, chickens and ducks along with a whole host of cats who knew exactly when to congregate outside the dairy for a drink at milking time.

When we were very busy I helped out with the other seasonal jobs. Dung spreading was still done by hand. A tractor, or the horses, carted loads out into the field and dumped it out in piles, and then a team of us would scatter it out with special hand forks, spreading it evenly across the field. It was hard work but always a fun occasion, with good camaraderie and banter. This particular task was frequently referred to by a selection of amusing, usually unrepeatable names, which varied depending on where in the country it was being performed and the dialect particular to the area.

Hay making was fun, a busy time relying on the weather to stay fine while it was being made, everyone came to help. The horses came in useful when the tractors were working flat out, so I used to take Jethro, who was the youngest horse, out with the hay rake to scratch up the last few wisps. Some of the fields were adjacent to the railway line, and Jethro hated and feared the noise and smoke from the steam trains. If one was coming by, I had to jump off and pacify him as he had been known to take off.

Harvesting was still done by cutting the corn then standing the stooks up for it to ripen, before putting it through the threshing machine. There were few combine harvesters at that time. When linseed was threshed it had to be put through twice to salvage all the very fine grain. I used to wet the straw from the wheat harvest and pull it into long, straight lengths for Bill when he thatched the hay and straw stacks to keep harsh winter weather out. Harvest suppers were still celebrated when all was safely gathered in.

Once we had moved in to Dairy Cottage, it was arranged that Mabel would feed me and two Danish men, Christian and Chris, who were in England on a year's exchange scheme to learn the language and our farming methods. They slept in the farmhouse where Pierre, a Swiss friend of the Chambers, and a German girl called Lisa also stayed. We were all in our early twenties and although we worked very hard, we played hard too. The tractor drivers and rest of the farm labour came from the village.

We belonged to the village darts team and used to practise madly on a darts board which we hung on a rather perforated larder door preparing for special tournaments at The Dorset Arms.

Withyham still had a railway station in those days which was just past the farm and sometimes if I was going to the pictures and was late, the old station master would hold the train for me if he saw me running down the road.

The Saturday night hop took place in the village hall once a month, which was quite a lively occasion. We were known as "The League of Nations" from Summerford Farm.

Once we all went to a fair in Tunbridge Wells where there was a hoopla stall. If you managed to throw a hoop to completely surround a bowl containing a goldfish, you won the fish. When the stallholders were busy chatting up the girls, the boys, who were tall and had long arms, reached over and placed hoops over three bowls. We came home with three goldfish who we christened Pip, Squeak and Wilfred.

Another night when the fish needed some fresh weed, we went down to the river. I was reaching down into the water to pull some out when one of the lads pushed me in. As I slipped into the water I managed to grab the culprit and took him with me. Much to the amusement of the others standing on the bank, we swam up the river fully clothed. It was the first and last time I ever swam wearing wellington boots.

I learned to wash jeans the Danish way. We took it in turns to do a major wash by giving them a good soaking in hot water, and then we laid them on the concrete outside the dairy and sprinkled them with soap powder. Using a yard broom, we gave them a good scrub, turned them over and did the same on the other side. Finally we hosed them off, gave them a final rinse in the dairy tank and hung them out to dry. It was a valuable lesson and years later I would adopt a very similar method when washing for a family who had perpetually dirty jeans!

One night when I returned home, the boys had done the ironing, including my under clothes. It was embarrassing seeing my bras plumped up neatly sitting on top of the pile! Apparently Mabel and Bill had watched them with great amusement.

The highlight for me when I remember my time at Summerford was when I showed Lyes Wild Emperor, the farm's pedigree Shorthorn bull at the big South of England show. I had to shampoo him from head to tail. He was a very large animal and seemed to quite enjoy the pampering. After I had hosed him off, I would fluff up all the parts that needed to make him look muscular and smooth down the rest of him. Hophurst Gracefull, a cow that also had to be prepared for the show, was not so keen on the shampooing session. As I was concentrating on scrubbing her hind legs, she lifted her tail, coughed and splattered me with warm, sticky manure.

Once at the showground, the animals had a stall each and I was given one too, as I had to sleep next to Emperor. He was very well behaved and didn't snore. The Herdsmen and women had a special marquee for food. Baked beans were dished up at every meal, enough to cause a gale force wind, so for a change of diet I decided I would try the posh, complimentary visitors' dining facility. I smartened myself up and marched to the door and explained to the steward that I was meeting somebody. He let me in and a waiter soon came to see what I would like. I ordered a roast and enjoyed the meal immensely. It was certainly an improvement on the baked beans!

I was so thrilled when Lyes Wild Emperor took first prize for Shorthorn bulls and also Best Bull in the show. Mr and Mrs Chambers were delighted and felt that all the hard work they had put in to build up their herd since their return to England from tea planting in India had paid off.

My days at Summerford were happy and sociable, and I have never forgotten my time there and the friends I worked and played with!

CHAPTER II

Approaching Twenty One

I was approaching my twenty first birthday and therefore out of parental control, so I made up my mind to look into schemes for agricultural students abroad. I wrote to various places and had an interview to explore the possibility of going to Canada or New Zealand, but the thought of a girl going off to work on a farm abroad on her own was frowned upon by the pleasant gentleman who interviewed me. He strongly advised me against it. Later I was given an address for a farm in Denmark and wrote to the farmer. The language was a problem and I discussed the matter with Chris, the older of the Danish students I was working with at the time, who said that he did not like the tone of the letter and that the farm was not in a good area, so I was back to square one. The Women's Land Army had been disbanded the previous year, which would have suited me and been a good experience. I was still keen on the idea of gaining more experience abroad and was putting out feelers. It seemed to be more a case of not what you knew, but who you knew.

I used to go home on my days off and George would usually be waiting for me en route at a pub near Ashdown Forest. It was flattering but at the same time of course I felt guilty that he was still interested in me, and I couldn't deny that I was becoming fond of him. George was horrified at the thought of me going abroad and tried to persuade me to change my mind. He was not very happy with his life at that time. I thought that was probably the tale many older men told young girls and that there was truth in the proverb that the grass on the other side of the fence always looked greener.

Biddy had warned me of his marriage problems, and I knew that there are always two sides to a story. When George's wife found out what was going on she came to see me at home, with my parents present. It was a most uncomfortable and unpleasant situation.

George and his wife Louise had two little girls Mary and Sheila. They had met when he was in the army in Scotland. She was Scottish, a school teacher, and five years older than him. Although I am sure they were very much in love at the time, George was a genius practically, but suffered from dyslexia, a condition where spelling the written word correctly causes difficulty. I later discovered that he had thought that a school teacher would make an ideal partner because she would be able to do the book-keeping, and also the more complicated paper work. Compatibility as life partners seemed to have come a poor second.

I knew how hard George worked and that he still longed for a son, but Louise did not want any more children. What I did not realise was that he was eyeing me up as a prospective broodmare. I seemed to have all the necessary qualifications; I was strong, well built and handy with both stock and tractors, I guess that he presumed some of those attributes must surely go through in the genes and any offspring we produced could provide a useful labour force in the future.

I had just had my twenty first birthday. There were no great celebrations, but I went home for the weekend and my parents gave me a solid gold watch and a copy of a brilliantly clever painting by Franz Halz, called The Laughing Cavalier from The Wallace Collection, which to this day I have always loved and treasured. Wherever you are in the room, the Cavalier's charismatic eyes are smiling at you.

One evening on the way home from work, George was waiting for me and we went to a pub in Ashdown Forest. I did not normally drink alcohol except for the odd glass of Woodpecker Cider, I usually just had lemonade. However, on this occasion I decided to try a drink that my sister had said was the very latest, fashionable drink, called Thunder and Lightning. It was cider mixed with gin. For someone who rarely drank it strangely blurred my vision and my defences became very relaxed.

A month or two later I discovered that I was pregnant. It took a while for the fact to sink in before I began to contemplate my future, rather difficult situation. George seemed quite happy and said he would stand by me, and sort something out, which was a great relief.

I decided not to tell my parents until it became obvious but in the meantime it would be better to work closer to Reigate and George. I therefore handed in my notice at Summerford Farm.

I managed to find a job nearer to home with a herd of Guernsey cows at Bridgeham Farm, Forest Green, near Dorking in Surrey. The farm was owned by Mr and Mrs Ehrenfeld, from Austria. He had been a General in the army and she bred poodles. They knew that I was pregnant and for the time I was there, they were incredibly good to me. They had a daughter who was living with her boyfriend, whom Mrs. Ehrenfeld referred to as her sin-in-law.

I lodged with the Farm Manager Fred, and his wife Mabel. They had a son in his early twenties who had just left home. I had porridge for breakfast every morning and one day my porridge was full of little black specks, which on closer examination proved to be mice droppings. Mabel's eyesight was not too good and she hadn't noticed that the larder had been invaded by mice, but the situation was swiftly brought under control by setting a few traps and keeping the oats in a closed container.

The Guernsey herd was easy to handle and with the help of two youngsters, Mary and Lenny, who had just left school, all went well. When it came to mucking out Lenny always said, in his cheerful Cockney accent, "Don't worry sweetheart, I'll empty the barrow for you."

It soon became impossible to hide my rapidly expanding girth. I will never forget my Mother's reaction when I plucked up the courage to tell her of my condition. At first, she froze on the spot, then finally burst out, "You wicked, wicked girl, how could you? Whatever do you think your Father will say? " I did not stop to find out but left my Mother to tell him. The next time I went home he confronted me and offered me the ultimatum, "You either have the baby adopted or get out." I had no difficulty in making the choice, which was to keep the baby and get out. It was a truly traumatic time but a decision that I have never regretted.

My Father, in the meantime, had retired from the Police force with twelve commendations for bravery for the handling of many difficult situations. He then worked as a Master at Arms for The Union Castle Line. Although he was away at sea for much of the time he left instructions to my Mother that I was not to set foot in his house. My Mother adhered to his wishes and I didn't go back home for over two years. It was after my Father's brother, my Uncle Fitz, came home from America and had a heart-to-heart with my dad that I was allowed back home again. During that time my Mother's family and my sister, who had been told to find lodgings elsewhere for coming in two minutes late after a party, were very supportive.

I worked at Bridgeham Farm until three weeks before Robert was born. I was fortunate to have found a very understanding doctor in Ewhurst, who actually remained our family doctor until sadly he was forced to retire due to Parkinsons Disease. We kept in touch until he died. He was the great-great nephew of Izambard Brunel, the designer of many famous bridges and the SS Great Britain, the first iron hulled steam ship.

George in the meantime had managed to purchase an old gypsy caravan and towed it forty miles along the road with wisps of smoke coming out of the chimney from hot ashes still smouldering in the little stove. He made a resting place for it beside some farm buildings owned by his father where there was running water and a toilet. We moved in and I spent the next three weeks cleaning and decorating it. It was a great relief that George's parents accepted me, and his Mother was very helpful, giving me advice as to what baby clothes to buy, along with all the other paraphernalia new babies needed. Fortunately they lived just half a mile away on their farm near Horley in Surrey.

In May 1955 Robert was born. George was thrilled to have a son, although as he glibly remarked, "What a shame he hasn't been born with his boots already on!" I had been used to rearing calves and other young animals but had no experience with young human beings. I had never done much cooking before either, let alone on an unpredictable old fashioned caravan stove, so it was all a bit of a shock.

George was not a "hands on" Father. He was of the opinion that children were still the woman's responsibility, which was the general attitude of the time, and it was taken for granted that after a hard day at work he would pop to the pub for a quick drink before coming home (to roost.) For the next six months a routine was established. I tried to have the meals nutritionally balanced and on time. Fortunately, Robert was a good, contented baby. I breast fed him every four hours and he spent all day outside under a tree in a large, old fashioned, second hand pram, watching leaves rustling in the breeze above him.

67

George's Father, who was very shrewd, looked for another farm for George and me to run. Farms belonging to the Broadwood Estate were for sale due to the death of the owner, who was renowned for making the famous Broadwood pianos. George and his father viewed several and they finally decided on Wattlehurst Farm. Although it was very run down, it looked to have the most potential as a dairy farm and was purchased for a very reasonable price. The fields at the highest point were on sandy soil which was quick drying and much better for early turn-out of livestock in spring and wet weather. The lower fields were heavy clay but fine for summer grazing. Before we moved in, we agreed that we should take a short break while we had the opportunity as it was the last chance before the years of hard graft that lay ahead. We took Robert and spent an idyllic week at Seaton in Devon.

CHAPTER 12

Wattlehurst Farm

On November 30th 1955, we moved to Wattlehurst Farm at Kingsfold, which is on the border of Surrey and Sussex, between Dorking and Horsham.

I will never forget the feeling of excitement and anticipation as we moved in. We drove up the long, rough drive, past the pond and as we rounded a bend, two deer shot into the wood. There on top of the hill, silhouetted by a breath taking panoramic view, stood the old dilapidated farmhouse that was to become my home. The original part of the house dated back to the 1500s. During the time we lived there, it was to reveal a little of its history.

We lived in an upstairs room for a month until the elderly couple who had been renting the farm moved out. From January 1st 1956 we were on our own – we took over from them lock, stock and barrel. There were 150 acres of mainly grassland, two large old barns, a cowshed and dairy, loose boxes, a cart shed and granary, plus two antiquated Fordson tractors. The livestock consisted of a small herd of milking cows, a few bullocks and a barn full of mangy, lice ridden battery hens together with a whole host of feral cats. We had what was known as a flying herd to start with; anything that didn't give enough milk and was not in calf had to go to market and was replaced by a more productive animal.

The framework of the original part of the house was constructed from massive oak beams, and the inside walls were wattle and daub. Wattles in Sussex were usually made from coppiced hazel which was split, then woven into whatever shape was required. The daub was a mixture of clay, horsehair and anything else considered suitable (including dung) mixed with water to make a workable plaster to cover the wattles. It was then usually lime washed. The advantage of wattle and daub construction was that it all expanded and contracted with the seasons. Some of these interior walls were still there. Inquisitive shoots from stinging nettles and various other plants would penetrate, emerging through gaps in the crumbling plaster.

Around the 1700s another four rooms had been added, possibly a conversion from a barn beside the house. At the end of the 1800s another four rooms were constructed. The roof had been leaking for many years and water had been running along inside, saturating the massive beams, many of which were believed to have been retrieved from derelict ships. Fungus was sprouting from them in many places.

Heart of Oak

Long ago in an ancient forest
Beside the storm tortured torso of the tree that bore it,
A tiny acorn grew.
Protected and drawn tall by surrounding trees,
Warmed by the sun, washed by the rain.
Transformed into a massive oak by centuries of seasons.
A solid, silent sentinel, witnessing man and beast.
Alas to be felled in its prime.

Limbs hewn and dragged asunder. Power and glory divested.
A skeleton of its former self, left to season.
Years later, trundled to the coast and
Cleaved into beams to form a mighty ship which
Sailed through storm and tempest, lashed by turbulent seas,
Floundered with priceless cargo in unfathomable depths,
Plundered by pirates, seared by tropical heat,
Finally returned to be broken, no longer seaworthy.

The massive timbers were once again trundled back in land.
Trussed, forming the framework of a cottage.
A puissant dwelling, guardian to generations.
Like a confident, never to reveal their secrets.

Their joys and sorrows echoing through the beams.
Ghosts from the past enchanting the present inhabitants.
A delight to historians living in a plastic world.
They call it Atmosphere.

Written on 24-2-1982 for English Literature homework at O-level class, Forest Boys School Adult Education Centre. Published as a runner up in the local paper's Poetry Contest.

It was written after having been searching for a subject to write about and inspiration finally came while gazing at the ancient beams holding the floor up above my head at Wattlehurst. I wondered at how such massive beams had once grown from a tiny acorn.

We soon discovered that in frosty weather the walls of the house, only one brick thick with no insulation, would glisten with ice inside.

Because the house sat on top of a hill, when the wind blew, which it frequently did with force, it used to whistle eerily through all the cracks and crevices, blasting snow and rain horizontally through various hidden cavities, as well as vertically through the roof. There was no electricity or gas but we did have the luxury of one tap of mains cold water in the house. We wore several layers of clothes to keep warm. I heated water in a rustic outhouse where there was a well and an old copper. The wood fire, which we lit underneath, supplied us with all the hot water for boiling our clothes and for filling buckets to carry into the house for washing and bathing. We went to bed by candlelight, which fascinated young Robert, who always wanted to grab the candle. We had an oil lamp in the hall, which cast shadows in the dark corners.

Tilly lamps lit the kitchen and cowshed. They ran on paraffin, at least they did when we managed to get them to light. All the furniture was second hand and old blankets made good draught-proof curtains to drape at the windows.

To start with, we made a temporary kitchen in the old dairy. The surrounding stone slabs made handy worktops. There was no damp course beneath the Sussex flagstone floor so the coconut matting we placed would usually be quite moist. Our best investment was a calor gas stove for cooking and a little heating. I was also able to dry nappies on the plate rack of the cooker in an emergency, taking great care not to set the house on fire. We had a bucket loo situated in the oldest part of the house. It was well out of the way and I found it a very creepy spot in the dark.

Having come from a relatively modern, centrally heated home, I found it quite an exciting challenge. Life was tough but in between milking and caring for all the animals, we gradually managed to pull things around. We made improvements and decorated the parts of the house that we lived in, but the kitchen was still the only room that had constant heating, so everything that needed to be kept dry was crammed in as orderly a fashion as possible in various cupboards. When we finally made a kitchen in the newer part of the house, George installed an old, wood burning Rayburn and much later, a second hand Aga cooker. Having a warm room, with somewhere to cook and dry clothes in winter was truly a transformation. George also bought an old, temperamental Petter generator which, when it was working, made enough electricity for a few lights. The rest of the house we gradually refurbished over the years, as best we could on a tight budget.

Robert continued to be a model baby, sitting in the cowshed strapped in his large, old- fashioned pram, playing with corn in plastic cups while I milked the cows.

When the walls in the bedroom glistened with frost on freezing cold mornings there were one or two occasions when the top cover of Robert's cot was crisp with ice. It must have been the nearest thing to having been in suspended animation but remarkably, he never caught a cold until he went to school.

However, it was not long before the model baby soon blossomed into the most inquisitive, venturesome child with unbelievably ingenious ideas. In no time at all it seemed he was toddling around. Each morning I would take him with me to check on the dry cows that were in the fields at the bottom of the farm and I would teach him their names. His favourite one was a friendly cow named Rose. On the way back to the farmyard we would look at all the different type of trees and inspect any interesting things going on in the hedgerows as the season changed. I would try to give simple explanations to his never ending questions and thought that he had understood. He would remain silent and look thoughtful for a moment, then say, " Mm, now you tell me all that again." When he had been with George one day helping to bring in a cow that had just calved, he told me that he didn't touch the calf, because "Its paint isn't dry"! Just outside the back door we made a fenced yard where Robert could play safely with his toys. One day, when it seemed rather quiet, I looked out to check. He had disappeared. My heart missed a beat when I discovered that he had managed to climb on a box and undo the gate. I hurried out calling his name. There was no reply. I rushed over to the pond nearby. I felt sick with worry as I scanned the pond for bubbles, thinking he might have fallen in. Then to my great relief, I heard a clatter and found Robert staggering out of the workshop with a can of paraffin. This was to be the first of his many escapades.

Joe, the collie dog who was one of the family, played his part; he liked to lie beside the pram as though guarding it. At milking time, George would shout "Go on back," and Joe would round up the cows and drive them up to the yard. Early in the mornings, while George drank his cup of tea, he would again shout "Go on back," and usually Joe would be waiting with the cows at the yard gate. Once in a while, George would go out and there would be no sign of Joe or the cows. It happened on odd, sporadic occasions which lasted several days on the trot. We later discovered the cause. When the bitch on the neighbouring farm was on heat, Joe had more important things on his mind than herding cows. He knew that he would quite literally be in the doghouse for his misdemeanours. I had watched him from the bedroom window, when he returned later in the day. He would craftily wait for George to go out of the house, and then he would slink up close beside the hedge and quickly disappear under the hall table onto his bed and clean himself up.

There was a certain ambience to the farmhouse. Frequently, I wondered who had lived there, all those years before us. It often felt as though I was not alone.

Now and again odd things would happen. The first was when I was busy painting a door in the old hall. It was a calm day, there was no wind blowing but it slowly opened towards me. I thought it was very weird but I was too busy to dwell on it.

It was not until we were trying to find a babysitter that we realised Wattlehurst was reputed to be haunted, nobody from the village wanted to oblige.

Gradually stories began to emerge – the first one being something about a girl drowning in a millpond. There were tales of the man who would never walk back home from the pub through Wattlehurst, because apparently a strange apparition opened the gates by the pond for him. Petrified by the experience, he took a much longer route home. There were many other tales of the gates opening and closing on their own. Another story was about five people visiting the farm one day, four of whom saw 'a ghost' on the drive but one did not. They arrived up at Wattlehurst very shocked and in need of resuscitation.

One night, when I was relaxing in my newly acquired bath and mulling over our next home improvement project, I heard the door to the empty, upstairs room creak open, then footsteps slowly walked across the floor above me and through into the next room. My heart missed a beat. I froze for a moment, then told myself not to panic; perhaps it was George? I did not linger long and grabbing a towel, I beat a hasty retreat upstairs, to find George fast asleep in bed. However, the next morning I asked him why he went up in the flat, as we called it. The reply was, "I never went up there last night, whatever would I want to go up there for? You must have been dreaming." He was not one to play tricks. I was puzzled by the experience but also quite intrigued.

We later became friendly with a local farmer, whose relations had farmed Wattlehurst up until 1922. They were able to tell us more. The ghost was said to be a very tall lady. She wore a lace veil and had been seen many times. She liked to blow the candles out on the piano and had been seen sitting on a chicken coop under the huge oak tree that stood in the field, on the way up to the house.

The stories fascinated me and as she had never harmed anyone, I began to feel she was a friendly soul and on occasions, I was definitely not alone.

Our busy life continued. When we later had started to breed greyhounds for racing, there were often up to fifty dogs demanding attention. As work increased, my friend Janet came to give me a hand in the house. Janet had a little girl called Joanne who used to play while her mother was busy with the chores. One day Joanne, who was about four years old, came into the kitchen and said, "Mummy, there is a lady in the hall." Janet was mortified as she realised who it was. When we looked, there was no-one there.

Sometimes at night, the greyhounds would all start howling. It sounded eerie, reminding me of the tale of The Hounds of the Baskerville. At first,

I just thought they were baying to the moon, perhaps calling the pack together. Sometimes they did it when there was no moon shining, so I would reckon it was because a bitch was coming on heat. On other occasions, there was no explanation as to what had set them going in the dead of night. I did just wonder... had they seen something strange?

One day, when John was about ten years old, he came in from the bathroom looking very pale and said, "Mum, I've just seen her." When I asked him who he had seen, he replied "The ghost." I calmly asked him what she had looked like. His childlike response was "Well, she was very high and her face was all cobwebby and she had no feet." We went to look for her but of course, she had disappeared. He had neither seen or knew what a lace veil was, so 'cobwebby' was the closest (and indeed apt) description he could think of to use.

I phoned the neighbour who knew what our ghost looked like and she confirmed that everyone else who had actually seen her had also described her as very tall, with a lace veil. John was not a lad to exaggerate and always called a spade a spade. To this day, he has never altered the description of what he saw.

A few more years passed and I was busy sorting out the washing in our utility room. There had once been an old bread oven in there. I no longer had to use the copper outside but had a washing machine, which saved an awful lot of hard work. If any water overflowed, it just used to percolate through the old stone slabs. We had never excavated beneath the floor. They were still the original stones – goodness knows how old they were. As I was loading up the machine, someone tapped me quite hard on the shoulder and startled me. I quickly swung round to find there was nobody there. I thought to myself that will be David, the vet I used to work for. We were expecting him to come out to look at a sick cow. He was a great practical joker, so I went outside to see if his car was in the yard. There was no car, so I went right out to the cow shed, but still there was no car. I thought it was exceedingly odd but could not work it out. Later when George came home for lunch, he told me what a narrow escape he had had. A huge lorry had just missed crashing into his car at a junction. I asked, "Was it at about twelve fifteen?" "Yes" he replied, "How do you know?" I told him what had happened, but he just shrugged his shoulders and shook his head. He was a man of few words.

Many years later, our neighbour phoned to say that their very elderly aunt who had seen the ghost, was visiting for the day. They wondered if she could come back and have a look at Wattlehurst, the farm where she had spent her childhood. That afternoon we lit the big open fire especially for her. We listened spellbound, as she sat there reminiscing, telling us all her stories; how she had seen the lady sitting on the chicken coop and how she had appeared to fancy one of her brothers, who had seen her on several occasions. Then she turned to me and said, "My dear, do you mean to tell me that you have lived up here for all these years and she has never tapped you on the shoulder?" Well, for once I was lost for words. Apparently, our ghost was renowned for startling people with a tap, just as I had experienced that day several years ago.

Once when John's friend Walter came to help us out, he slept up in the old part of the house and experienced something strange but wishing to preserve his reputation as a tough man, he was too embarrassed to tell anyone that he had seen a ghost. He later told John in confidence what had taken place.

We still hear the odd rumour about her. Is it mere coincidence that several sightings and descriptions of her correspond? Is there any possible reason why some selected individuals experience the ghostly "tap on the shoulder"? There is no apparent explanation for these occurrences. However, very curiously, several years ago while excavation work was being undertaken, some circular foundations were unearthed which bore resemblance to the base of an old mill. We knew there were dew ponds close to this discovery; could one of these have been known as the "mill pond" reputed to be the location of the unfortunately lady's demise? It is my firm belief that in the not too distant future quantum physics or a related branch of science will prove a relationship between the dissipation of energy after death and the phenomena we currently describe as paranormal activity. When that time comes we will have a better understanding of how and why the mysterious lady watches over the residents of Wattlehurst.

I live at the bottom of Wattlehurst drive now. To date, she has not ventured down this far. I can see the old house from my window, when on occasions I wander up the drive, past that ancient oak tree, that has stood for centuries, like a silent sentinel, a confidant, alone in the field by the house, I muse to myself, if only it could talk.

In 1957 George developed a fistula and was admitted to hospital for an operation. My old school friend Ena and her husband Don, who was a farm manager came to stay, as fortunately they could spare the time prior to his starting a new job. It worked out well, and they kindly helped out until George was out of hospital and fit again.

In 1957 my Uncle Fitz returned home to the UK, having spent many years in South America, and he stayed with my parents. He had a heart to heart talk with my father and persuaded his brother to forgive me for my past behaviour. I remember how overjoyed I was when, one beautiful sunny afternoon, the three of them came to see us. It was the first time I had seen my parents since I had left home two years previously. Although a little uncomfortable at the beginning, the reunion went well as everyone relaxed and chatted together. Robert, who was two and a half, met his grandparents for the first time. We all had a walk around the farm and my parents and Uncle Fitz took some photos of a happy family afternoon, and I soon felt as though all had been forgiven.

Later that evening my uncle took George down to the pub for a drink. My Father didn't go with them as he drank very little alcohol and in any case had to drive home. The most my parents ever had at home was a bottle of Woodpecker Cider shared between us, with Sunday lunch. Imagine my horror when the two of them finally came home from the pub. Uncle Fitz came in and was perfectly sober, but when George didn't come in my heart sank as I suspected the reason for his absence. I went outside and found him staggering beside the granary. My blood instantly rose to boiling point and anger welled up inside me. How could he have behaved like that, just as things were beginning to go so well between my Father and me? Was he completely unaware how important the afternoon's reconciliation with my parents was to me? I was so furious and without stopping to count to ten gave him one almighty thump – he overbalanced and landed in an undignified heap on the ground. He struggled to his feet and later staggered into the kitchen, bearing a cut to his head which was bleeding slightly. My mother almost had hysterics, saying that she was not used to such behaviour. My Father looked disgusted and Fitz apologised profusely for having bought him too many drinks. The reunion I had so welcomed had come to an end in the worst way possible. As for George – he could remember nothing the next morning, but it did take quite a while for my blood pressure to return to normal and even longer for me to forgive him.

As soon as we could afford to do so, we employed a young lad from the village to help out on the farm. His name was Ian and he drove a little bubble car. Robert christened it, "Igam's Bubble." One glorious summer morning in1958 George suggested that we should take a well earned day off to go to the seaside now that Ian was able to milk the cows.

We had a great day. Robert had his first paddle in the sea and made sand castles. On the way home the sky became hazy with a strange orange glow. It looked as though a storm was brewing. When we arrived home, George went outside to check everything was in order, and when he came in he said to shut all the windows. The sky became black and the birds stopped singing as it grew darker. Leaves began to rustle as a breeze started to blow. It felt strange and looked as though the storm was about to break any minute. Then we heard the first ominous rumbles in the distance. Within minutes, the violent, whirling, vortex of a hurricane force storm hit us. We were engulfed by the howling gale, while huge hailstones which settled like snow were accompanied by terrifying forks of lightening shooting to earth in the front garden. We sat in the kitchen, me petrified and George was worried too but we tried not to let it show in case it upset Robert, who was looking a little apprehensive. Then there was an almighty clatter as the hailstones broke the upstairs windows, which took the full force of the gale. The deluge of wind and hail caused part of the ceiling to cave in. The storm seemed to last for an eternity but it must have all been over in less than an hour. We were very relieved it was over and that we were unscathed, with just the aftermath to deal with.

The storm was recorded as a tornado. The neighbouring farm lost several cows which had been struck by lightning. Many properties in the West Sussex area suffered major damage. It was noted in the Guinness Book of Records that the largest hailstones ever known in the UK fell in Horsham. They were the size of tennis balls and dented many cars. It took a long time for all the damage to be repaired and for life to resume as normal.

CHAPTER 13

The Joys of Motherhood

The warmest place in the house (apart from the kitchen) was in bed. With no television to watch either, it wasn't long before David was on the way. He arrived in January 1958, weighing 10lbs all but an ounce. He was not quite such a contented baby as Robert had been, as he suffered from eczema and asthma. The poor little chap had to wear gloves so that he didn't scratch himself raw. After he was weaned we discovered that he was allergic to cows' milk, providing me with the perfect reason to keep a goat again. Goats' milk is more easily digestible and we were hopeful it would suit David, so we acquired Lucky. Fortunately it paid off, her milk suited David well and his eczema dramatically improved. Lucky was a real character who quickly became one of the family. On wet days she would come into the kitchen to be milked. She enjoyed extra titbits and on one occasion, Robert encouraged her to pull a packet of cereals off the kitchen table. She thrust her head into the packet and walked around with it on her head devouring all the contents, much to his amusement.

One evening when I had put David and Robert, who was then almost four years old, to bed, I crept back upstairs to check that all was well. To my horror I found Robert sitting in the middle of his bed with the covers over his head, with a box of matches trying to illuminate his improvised tent! We thought we had been so careful putting all the matches for candles and the lamps out of reach; how wrong we were.

Once David was out of his pram and toddling, he became a bundle of mischief. He loved to help us collect the eggs. One day Robert was learning to count by carefully picking the eggs up one at a time from the nesting box, reciting each number as he put them into the basket. David watched for a while but he decided it was much more fun to grab the eggs from the nest boxes and smash them on the ground. Joe the dog obviously agreed with David's idea as he followed along behind, gobbling up all the broken eggs.

I was becoming a keen gardener and very proud of my first attempt to grow tomatoes. They were just starting to turn red, and I was eagerly looking forward to picking them, anticipating their flavour once they were ripe and had become fat and juicy. However one day when they were close to being perfectly ready to harvest, I discovered that David had beaten me to it and picked them and scattered them around while I was busy weeding another patch of garden!

When Robert was five, he started at Warnham School. He had to catch the school bus from Kingsfold. George would give him a lift down to the end of the drive when he took the milk churns down to the churn stand, ready for collection by the dairy. Robert would then wait for the bus with the other children from Kingsfold. The bus was usually driven by its owner, a lady in her eighties, who was well known for driving in the middle of the road. Miraculously, the children all arrived safely, and on time, for school. One day not long after Robert started school, he came home very angry because he had been severely reprimanded for peeing on a rose bed in full view of the road. Having only a bucket loo at home, he had always been encouraged to relieve himself outside, thus saving the effort of emptying the bucket too often. He hadn't discovered that the school had flushing toilets available.

David meanwhile would happily play on his little trike while his big brother was at school. The trike had a box on the back where he would squirrel away all sorts of little treasures. He would park the trike in the woodshed at night and we always knew that when things went missing, often including kitchen utensils, they could probably be found in his secret trike box. On one occasion David found an almost empty can of green paint. He made the most of the remains by painting artistic daubs everywhere, including on himself.

In June 1959, between haymaking and harvesting, George and I were able to snatch a few days holiday in Jersey. It was a wonderful break, made possible by my parents who came to look after the two boys.

Soon after Robert started school, (and nine months after our Jersey holiday!), John was born. It was Springtime and George was very busy when I went into labour, but nevertheless I was slightly taken aback when he asked if I could catch a bus to the hospital. Because he was used to calving cows I think he assumed that human beings were not much different. In the end he did manage to find the time to take me, dropped me off at the hospital door and sped off home. The nurses were surprised and wondered how I had arrived as I burst through the door, a little bow legged! John arrived shortly afterwards, weighing in at 7lbs 14oz. That evening when George came to see me, he was clutching a beautiful bunch of primroses that he had picked in the woods. Then, inevitably, he went off to wet the baby's head.

We had a new student named Brian who came to work on the farm. He had an adversity towards the electric fence which was used for strip grazing. Every day the fence had to be turned off while it was moved to create a fresh strip of grazing for the cows. Once it was turned on again, it had to be tested. Robert knew how to test it; when he held a very thin blade of grass on the wire it gave him a mild shock and he knew it was working properly. He had also learnt that if he tested it with anything larger than a thin blade of grass, it would produce a mighty shock. Brian, who had learnt the hard way, used to take five year old Robert out to test the fence for him. In the winter the gateways became like a quagmire where the cows walked through, so Brian carried Robert over the boggy parts. Unfortunately, on one occasion, Brian overbalanced and dropped Robert face-down in the mud. We heard a loud bellowing and when we looked out, we saw a strange, brown apparition staggering across the field, heading for the house. It was Robert, completely covered in mud. David had wondered what was making all the bellowing noise and was amused to find that, once we had peeled off his clothes and washed him off, his big brother was revealed.

Brian was not very competent and didn't stay with us for very long. He had been lodging with us in the house and I swear he went to bed with his boots on as he left a trail of mud everywhere, including up to his bedroom. He was unbelievably untidy and he had an enormous appetite – it was like trying to fill a bottomless pit. I was quite sure that he needed worming!

Our next student was Frankau, a Hungarian who had managed to escape from the communist rule of his homeland. His English was not very good, and George and he did not understand one another very well. We discovered on investigation of a strange, pitter-pattering noise coming from above our loo that Frankau was rearing young chickens in his bedroom. He was not impressed when we explained that usually we kept them outside in our country.

David was intrigued with his baby brother John and long before John could even sit up, had to be discouraged from putting little toy lorries and cars, grubby from the sandpit, into the pram to amuse John. They later played happily together most of the time, although I needed eyes at the back of my head to watch what they were getting up to.

The playpen I had used for all the boys did not have a base to it. It unfolded and sat straight on a blanket on the floor. John was ingenious from very early on. He found a way to escape by wriggling out underneath. He also found a way to climb out of his cot. I found that by moving the cot to a position in front of the wardrobe mirror kept him amused. He was fascinated as he watched the image of himself. I did wonder whether it would have an adverse effect in the long term, but it worked fine at the time. As John grew up he became very interested in how everything worked. His first favourite toy was an old coffee percolator. He would fill it with sand or water and loved to watch it filtering through as he poured it out.

On David's first day at school he was very happy to play with all the cardboard money, and when he arrived home in the evening with his pockets stuffed full of it he quite thought that he had become rich very quickly. He was so disappointed when we told him that it really belonged to the school and it all had to be returned.

My life was full with three little boys to look after as well as cooking for the family and helping out with farm work. I had also to deal with George's requirements. He would go down to the pub for a pint dead on 12 o'clock each day, and again in the evening for an hour or two. Lunch had to be sharp at 1 o'clock and supper at 9 o'clock. He was a stickler for time and I tried to fit in with his routine as best I could.

I was very unhappy one day when George announced out of the blue that his mates at the pub had invited him to join them on a trip to Ireland for a few days. Although there was someone available to milk the cows, I was expected to hold the fort and would be responsible if anything went wrong. Unfortunately, a message to tell the tanker driver to come up to the farm to collect the milk, instead of the usual arrangement to pick up from a churn stand at the end of the drive, had not been passed on. I had a heated confrontation with the driver who was forced to make a return journey especially to pick up our milk. Fortunately everything else went well and there were no disasters to speak of.

When George returned from Ireland, he was surprised when I announced that I would be going off for a few days myself. I had booked to go to Butlins at Bognor, despite the advice of booking staff that taking three children on my own would not be easy. I was determined to go nonetheless.

On the first day we were there, I was unpacking my suitcase and Robert went out to play on a little roundabout. Somehow in his enthusiasm for speed, Robert managed to trap his foot underneath as the roundabout spun, causing a nasty laceration which needed daily treatment and dressing at the clinic. It wasn't the best start to my holiday.

I went to the restaurant on site for meals, taking David and Robert inside with me and leaving John strapped in his pram, carefully positioned by the window so I could keep an eye on him.

While on our little holiday, I thought about the fact that my Mother had questioned me several times as to whether the children were to be christened. I was not too keen on the idea as I had always thought that children should be free to make up their own minds once they were old enough to study and understand the ways of the world. However, I decided that whilst at Butlins there was a golden opportunity to have the three boys christened as a job lot, and in the process my Mother would be happy. I discussed the situation with the Vicar, who was a pleasant, understanding man and the arrangements were made and they were all duly christened. While I was thanking the Vicar following the ceremony, we discovered that David had disappeared. Several older children playing nearby, known at the camp as Beavers, were sent to look for him. A little while later he was found happily playing on a big roundabout, ringing its bell while pretending to be a train driver.

Another morning, John managed to slam the door of the chalet shut while I was sorting out his pram, leaving him inside with the keys and me locked outside. I had to send Robert off to find a Redcoat with a key to let me in. In the meantime I had to chat to John through the letterbox, hoping that he didn't do anything drastic while I waited for the Redcoat to arrive. The holiday was definitely a little hectic but it was fun, and I enjoyed the company of a mixed bunch of human beings for a change.

Life resumed in an orderly routine once I had settled back from my holiday at Butlins. George would come in for his breakfast at 7.30 a.m., then Robert would go off to school and I would take David and John out to feed and check the stock. The boys would try to help, then later when they were tired out I would put them to bed for a sleep, giving me time to get on with household chores and have lunch ready on time. In the afternoon they would play together while I did my rounds, at the same time as trying to keep an eye on what they were getting up to. When Robert came home from school we would have tea. Around 6.30 p.m. they took turns to have a bath in the kitchen sink, as it was some time before we had hot running water in the bathroom. After their bath, it was upstairs to bed. I always read them a story before they went to sleep and they had usually nodded off by 7.30 p.m. I was then able to sort out their clothes for washing, do any ironing and maybe make soup or pies for the next day.

Sometimes Sunday afternoons saw the routine varied when we would go to our parents for tea, or they would come to see us.

Robert was doing well at school. He was lucky to have a teacher who encouraged him to read. He was always keen to try and answer questions. Apparently in a Scripture lesson one day when the class was asked how they carried water in the time of Jesus, Robert suggested a plastic bag would be more practical than one made from goatskin!

David was a thoughtful lad. When the weather was cold and wet, he took some of the tiny, unwanted home grown carrots and left one at each rabbit burrow he could find as a Christmas present for the bunnies, and he really entered into the spirit of Christmas by decorating the Christmas tree with tampax that he had found in a box in the store cupboard, which he thought were little crackers.

John had been craftily helping himself to my home made mincemeat. He had discovered it while it was maturing in a cupboard. It had to be stirred each day for a week before potting it up. Half of it was missing when that time came. The following Christmas I made sure it was well hidden!

CHAPTER 14

Good and Bad Times

In September 1962, my 4th baby was two weeks overdue and the gynaecologist at Dorking Hospital thought that it would be wise to induce the birth, which they did. Richard was born weighing 7lbs 14ozs. Following the rapid birth, I suffered a massive haemorrhage. An emergency doctor was called and he and his medical team fought to save my life. I was later told that I had lost over half the blood in my body in ten minutes. I remember feeling as though my life was ebbing away – the team around me became distant and hazy, their voices sounded strange as though I was under water. Later, I awoke to find myself alone in a room where my body was lying on the bed but I seemed to be floating above it. This weird sensation continued on through the night. I dropped off to sleep for a while but every time I woke up, I was still floating above, trying to join my body. The next morning, once they had information on my blood group, I was given a blood transfusion. Gradually, I came back together again, although I was very weak.

Richard was fine. George had been worried, but in those days fathers were not allowed to attend a birth. A fortnight later I returned home and tried to pick up the threads again. George was very supportive in the week that followed, but I couldn't cope. My body had taken a battering and I had post natal depression, which was horrendous. I felt as if I was in a black hole with no way out.

I went back into hospital and slowly, over the next few weeks, I managed to crawl out of the black hole. My mother and father looked after the two youngest and George's parents looked after David. Robert went to the parents of Ian (the lad with the bubble car who had worked for us). They lived in Warnham village, so Robert was still able to attend school. He was very excited when one night while he was staying there, Tiger, the cat, produced a litter of kittens on his bed.

When I returned home, George had found me a temporary housekeeper. She was a homely, middle aged lady named Jean, who had a teenage daughter. She helped me look after the family for a while, until Ian's brother Colin married Janette. The couple came to live in the flat above the farmhouse, so she was on hand to help me with the four very lively youngsters. This worked out well.

George had installed a new, reliable Listomatic generator so we had electricity everywhere and at last there was no need for candles or Tilly lamps. It was a great leap forward, the only drawback being when someone forgot to turn any of the lights out behind them, as the generator didn't stop until the last light was turned off. On the odd occasion, having snuggled down in bed, weary, after a hard day's work, the generator would still be chugging merrily away, which meant that some brave soul had to rise again to turn it off. It was no joke on a cold winter's night, especially if the offending light was outside, in which case an old coat over nightclothes was required.

With Janette and Colin occupying the flat, George bought an old caravan for the various students we had working for us to live in. I continued to feed them. They were a very mixed bunch. One was mad on fishing, another had a pet ferret that ran around in the kitchen while he had his dinner. There was one who was light fingered and had been in trouble with the law, another had spent time at an approved school in Surrey, and coincidentally had been blessed with the same wonderful headmaster and his wife who had been at Sheephatch School in Tilford when I was there twelve years earlier. Mr and Mrs Gould had moved and taken on the very difficult challenge of the approved school, and with their amazing ability with young people, had gone on to straighten out the lives of some very difficult youngsters. I kept in touch with them until they died.

Our two local lads were great. One of them was later killed in a tragic motor accident. His father and another relation continued to do maintenance work for us at weekends for many years and could turn their hands to almost anything. They had come from a family of well diggers.

They would first divine for the water and then miraculously build the wells, brick by brick from the top down, some to great depths.

As the milking herd increased in size and made a profit, more reliable, daily help was required, so a Woolaways pre-cast bungalow was built at the end of the drive for a cowman. This relieved the pressure all round. I no longer had to feed ravenous teenagers.

In 1964 George's father died, so his mother came to stay with us for a while, until we built another bungalow for her to live in beside the cowman's. She told us many stories about her childhood, including how her ancestors had been Keepers of The Heraldry and that a King had given them land on the outskirts of London, named South and North Mimms, Mimms being her family name.

Joe, the collie, was getting old and not too keen to round up the cows, so George bought another collie, called Bingo. The two dogs fought at every opportunity. Bingo was too fast so George tied one foot up to slow him down, but that didn't really work. Eventually he gave Bingo to our neighbour, who owned the local cattle lorry. Bingo lived a life of luxury and could be seen proudly sitting up in the passenger seat, looking out of the window as they drove to the markets. Joe was relieved and quite liked Jane, a pedigree labrador, that Robert trained as a gun dog.

It was a tradition in George's, and indeed in many farming families, that boys were given a gun as soon as they were old and responsible enough to shoot. Robert was nine years old and very proud of his 4-10 gun and Jane, his dog. She later absconded one dark night when she was in season, and had an illicit liaison with the cowman's dog, which looked like a labrador with a dash of doberman pincer. Nine weeks later a litter of puppies arrived, one of which was Tara, a real character, who later helped to train the greyhounds to chase. She was big and strong and looked quite formidable but was petrified of thunder and used to dive into a dark corner, trembling, at the first sign of a storm. I often stayed with her as I too didn't like thunder.

CHAPTER 15

The Greyhound Era

In the 1960s I acquired my first greyhound bitch from Joe, who was a friend of George. Joe was seriously keen on greyhound racing and owned several dogs. George liked to go racing with him and decided that he would like to own a racing greyhound too. His first venture was with a dog called Easily Led that he purchased from an Irish priest for a considerable amount of money. Unfortunately, the dog turned his head while racing, which meant that he would challenge any dog racing close beside him, instead of chasing the electric hare. They are always disqualified for such behaviour and if lucky, this could lead to enforced retirement and a life of luxury on someone's couch. However, the outcome could be far less fortunate if the dog fell into unscrupulous hands as, according to an Irish expression, he was likely to end his days "thanks to a little lead in his left ear"!

I thought that it would be a sensible idea to have a go at breeding our own dog, rather than pay an exorbitant price for a genuine, top class racing dog, so when Joe offered to give George a well bred greyhound bitch named Jenny Lind, who had been mated several times but remained barren, I jumped at the chance to have another try with her.

I consulted David, the vet that I used to work for. The next time she came into season, he gave her a hormone injection and she had to be mated much further on in her heat than an average bitch. Nine weeks later, making up for lost time, she surprised us all by producing a huge litter of sixteen puppies. Sadly, two were born dead and the remaining fourteen I separated, marking half with green dye and half with red. That way I was able to give them to Jenny in two shifts, making sure that she gave them all a good feed and did not miss giving any a good stimulating clean. She was an excellent mother and to keep the milk flowing, she had a balanced feed every four hours. I introduced the puppies to solid food early and kept them warm under an infra-red lamp, and miraculously she managed to successfully rear them all. Two tiny ones I gave away as pets at nine weeks old, and later I sold eight and kept four to rear on. The four I kept became top class Open Racers, and my enthusiasm for breeding racing greyhounds was complete. Jenny had several more very successful litters and when retired she became a much loved pet.

I began to breed and rear dogs for other people. My experience working with vets and with animals in general became very valuable. At one time I had up to fifty greyhounds of different ages, each with their own character and personality to be catered for, and over the next twenty years the breeding and care of the dogs was a hugely enjoyable and important part of my life, and a lucrative hobby that fitted in well with family life and rearing my little boys.

George too was enthusiastic and converted some of our outhouses into kennels. We had a small brick building right beside our back door which became known as "Maternity Ward 10". Using a large old door, a hammer, planks of wood and my favourite four inch nails, it was easy to construct an ideal whelping bed. The old door was set up on bricks to keep it up off the floor and away from draughts and four wide planks of wood made it deep enough to stop tiny puppies climbing over. Thick wads of newspaper made the best bedding as the print had slight antiseptic properties and it was easy to tear off the pages as they became soiled. An adjustable infra-red lamp was placed at one end and the bitch could choose to lie under or away from the heat.

The puppies would be led out by their mothers while they were still young, a litter at a time. Once they were weaned and old enough, the litters were split up. They were reared outside in small, warm sheds filled with clean straw, deep enough for them to make cosy nests, along with large pens outside to play in. They had to be matched for pecking order. The bullies were put with each other or an older dog, so as they grew they finished in compatible pairs. Later Tara, our Labrador-cross bitch, used to take them across the fields. Being part retriever she liked to carry something in her mouth, so she happily held a pair of old tights. The puppies would race after her trying to grab the legs of the tights as they stretched out, waving in the breeze which was an amusing spectacle to watch as well as a wonderful way to teach them to chase.

The one drawback with greyhounds was that once they were chasing they hunted by sight and had an inherent pack instinct. When they were out for exercise they considered anything that moved as prey and gave chase. All cats, chickens and other small animals had to be locked up when excited greyhounds were let loose for their daily gallop across the fields.

On Sundays, the owners of the puppies I had sold and was rearing for them would often come to see how they were progressing. I had to be up at crack of dawn to make sure that the house and dogs were clean and tidy. The owners loved to take their dogs out for exercise across the fields. On their return the dogs would go back into their various pens and I would revive the often exhausted owners with cups of tea, coffee and biscuits. They were an interesting, very diverse bunch of characters, many of whom came down from London and the surrounding area. Some were very rich and others, not quite so affluent, owned dogs by forming syndicates. They were all friendly and as well as plenty of chat, much networking and wheeling and dealing of their wares took place between themselves. Some were into horse racing, others were car dealers and many had shops. Whatever their occupation, they all appeared to have had plenty of spare cash to play with. Some would accompany George down to the local pub to round off their visit.

The greyhound activity led to my first foray into book-keeping. I had to keep a meticulous account of outstanding costs, including those for worming the dogs, vaccinations and vet fees and produce invoices to be settled on the Sunday visits. At Christmas time, or when the dogs won, our family was spoilt as many generous owners brought gifts.

As the puppies grew, they had large appetites which had to be catered for. Each week I used to take a trip to a slaughterhouse near Gatwick Airport to buy meat from animals that were not fit for human consumption which, by law, had to be dyed. I would have several big plastic bins filled mainly with tripe, liver and sometimes horse meat, especially if there had been animals injured or on rare occasions, struck by lightning. I used to buy sacks full of carefully selected wholemeal bread from my brother- in-law who collected bread and cakes from London bakeries in a huge old pantechnicon lorry to feed the hungry pigs he kept.

The puppies had bread and milk in the mornings and a hopper full of special dog cereal midday. The meat was cooked in a large, antiquated electric wash boiler and which, when mixed with the bread and the gravy, made a wonderful balanced evening meal.

Vaccinations and worming had to be kept up to date and every dog had to be marked up for a passport, with every tiny mark detailed and then signed by a vet, who then tagged the dog with a number which was registered with The Greyhound Racing Association. No dog was allowed to race before it was 16 months old. Young greyhounds are known as saplings and it was important not to give young pups too much exercise, especially while their bones were still growing fast.

The thick wire mesh of the pens had to be six feet high as some of the dogs were capable of clambering up and jumping over. Others would manage to dig their way out underneath. If any were lame, I would sometimes let them run loose when all the others were penned in. They would soon come sound again, taking just as much exercise as they wanted. Now and again there would be real wimps wanting extra attention. They would cleverly refuse to put their recovered injured feet to the ground or pretend to still be lame. The solution was to bandage the other foot up, which usually worked like a miracle.

Once or twice a week, when they were ready to really stretch out (usually at about fourteen months old), we used to give them what was known as a "pipe opener". To increase their lung capacity, we encouraged them to chase an old fur hat attached to a cord, which had been taken to the bottom of the field by someone who could walk in a very straight line down to the traps. Once the dogs were focused and raring to go, the hat was dragged back up to the top of the field by someone with strong arms turning the wheel of the winder. They ran alone to start with, then in pairs, starting from a dual trap similar to the stadium ones. They loved galloping up to the top, flat out.

At sixteen months old they were ready for racing, having grown tough, big and strong, unlike some of the more unfortunate ones who arrived for training looking like rashers of wind. They resembled tender little greenhouse plants; sadly undernourished, full of worms and reared in small pens often in someone's back yard with little or no exercise.

At first our dogs were put with trainers at tracks all over the south of England. Later George took out a trainer's licence, so that we could train some of our own. A special race was held down at Brighton where all the dogs in the race came from one litter that we had bred. Another one from the same litter won the best racing bitch at the Wimbledon dog track in 1964. Her name was, Wattlehurst Lightening. But the most memorable evening was when Wattlehurst Rogue won the Wimbledon Puppy Derby in1968, beating many top Irish bred dogs in the trials leading up to the final.

I later reared another Wimbledon Derby winner: he was a real character named Rurakura Mutt. He had arrived from Ireland as a young puppy and belonged to a well known Brighton bookie.

They were exciting times. Having found a young, newly married couple to live up in the flat to baby-sit for us, I was able to dress for the occasions and go to some of the bigger races. I seldom put more than a small, each-way bet on any dog, but I enjoyed the banter and camaraderie and the meals in the restaurants. I was most intrigued at what was produced from under the counter and behind the scenes by ladies who served behind the bar at one of the smaller London tracks, which now no longer exists. It was the time of an influx of some rather suspect contraband coming in from abroad. There appeared to be little that could not be ordered. Parcels would mysteriously be handed over, having been retrieved from under the counter, especially in the way of cheap clothes and jewellery. It was an eye opener to me and a far cry from farming.

Tracks that did not belong to The Greyhound Racing Association, were called flapping tracks and it was known that some could be a little dodgy. I think that's why, in the past, Greyhound Racing had been christened The Sport of Knaves, presumably in ironic contrast to Horse Racing being referred to as The Sport of Kings.

It was possible at the flapping tracks in those days, to bribe the hare driver to drive a fast or a slow hare, depending on which trap favoured certain dogs, or if a wide runner was put in the inside trap, it would often impede the others trying to get to the outside. It had also been known that years ago a mat that slipped was sometimes secretly put in to give the opposition a bad start.

Dogs were kennelled separately before a race. If it was expected to win, it stood a much better chance if it had been tethered to stop it leaping up and down with excitement when it heard the hare in the previous races.

If it was not expected to win, it was left to go berserk when it heard the hare, so would have lost a considerable amount of energy before the race.

At all the licenced tracks everything was above board and carefully checked.

Each dog had to be weighed and was not allowed to vary more than two pounds from its last race weight. A vet was always in attendance to check each animal's passport, and was available in case of injury.

Dogs that were not suitable for track racing were often taken coursing, the sport they were originally bred for and now illegal in the UK. In coursing the dogs were held in pairs: one wore a red collar, the other a white. They were then released together to chase a live hare and it was the way they twisted and turned the hare that scored them their points, more than the actual kill.

I became fascinated by certain bloodlines in the greyhound pedigrees, especially observing various traits that went back many generations, and understanding their importance. Later we kept our own Stud Dogs and used to take in bitches for mating.

While all this was happening the boys were growing up, being part of everything that was going on, having plenty of space and freedom to do their own thing, frequently learning from their mistakes!

CHAPTER 16

Flexible Boundaries

In the winter of 1963, Kingsfold was cut off by the snow which left the main A24 road impassable. George managed to keep our drive clear by driving up and down with the tractor every few hours, day and night. He supplied churns full of milk to the village pub, which was at that time named The Wheatsheaf, where grateful villagers were able to trudge through the snow to collect it. It was several days before the road was cleared. The boys were in their element, having great fun playing in the snow.

Richard, who became known as Ricky, was a good baby. Early one morning when he was a few months old, George was out milking the cows and I was still in bed when I heard Robert, who was always an early bird, shuffling down the stairs. I went to investigate and found Robert and David trying to give Ricky his bottle which they had filled full with fizzy lemonade. It was with the best of intentions; they thought they would let me lie in. After a good burp Ricky was none the worse for the experience. He walked at ten months old, but being mobile so early was not such a good thing. He resembled a mischievous little monkey and spent his first years trying hard to keep pace with his brothers who, on the whole, were very good with him.

It was difficult keeping an eye on what they were all getting up to. On a farm there are so many interesting things to do and experiment with. It was a delicate balance not to set boundaries that were too rigid which may have stifled their enthusiasm to learn hands-on how things worked, but to ensure they understood the ever present dangers of farming life. I remembered the words of an old headmaster who had said at a lecture for parents that "A child is like a tree. You should allow it to grow naturally but prune out the undesirable parts and cup and jug the rest by pouring in the knowledge". There were also the old adages "Give me the boy until he is seven and I will show you the man" and "A boy will never be a man until he can do everything for himself", and last but not least "Manners maketh man". I endeavoured to do my best.

I will never know how all four boys reached manhood unscathed. Over the next fifteen years, life was never dull. They had to work hard to earn their pocket money and learnt to do all the various farm duties, along with household chores, including cooking. Every morning before school they had to clean their shoes. In the school holidays I would make out a rota of the jobs to be done, and when they were older they had to wash their own rugby kits.

Punishment was to work without wages and if the misdemeanours were really bad, there was always the threat of George's horse whip or my magic wand, which was a swishy hazel stick that lived on top of the cupboard in the kitchen. Although it mysteriously disappeared from time to time, replacements were always available from a large hazel bush which grew in the garden.

Most of the time while the boys were growing up we had friendly, reliable couples living in the flat, once we had made it habitable. They were able to give me a hand with the chores and double up as babysitters instead of paying rent. Two of these couples in particular have remained lifelong friends; Janet and Colin and Peta and Tony.

We met Colin and Janet through Colin's parents, who used to babysit for us from time to time. Janet's help in the house when the boys were young was a Godsend. Peta and Tony came to us while they were students looking for accommodation and Peta too helped enormously, especially in the task of getting the lunch on the table in time – it had to be dead on 1 o'clock!

One night when I had left the babysitters in charge, everything seemed fine when we returned home, but the next morning when I was doing my rounds I found that Robert's bedroom windowsill was sticky when I went to open the window. On closer inspection I found it had been freshly painted over with white paint, which appeared to have big black smears incorporated in it. When I asked John what had been going on he said he couldn't tell me, fearing that Robert would kill him. When Robert came clean – after similar life threats – it turned out that he had hidden some of the Guy Fawkes rockets and fired them out of the window which had left burn scars on the windowsill, so he had painted it over. He narrowly escaped the death penalty!

At weekends we had two retired farming friends who came to carry out various repairs. One day they found all four boys had climbed up on to the barn roof. They talked four year old Ricky safely down. Robert was very cheeky to them but they soon calmed him down by using a good old fashioned method; they put him in a large two and a quarter hundredweight wheat sack and hung him up on a hook. It was some time before Robert repented, apologised and showed some respect, at which point he was released. The lesson learnt that day lasted a lifetime.

John broke an arm jumping off hay bales and later broke the other one when an engine starting handle kicked back. He also had to be whisked off to hospital to have a gash above his eye stitched up when he had been throwing paper darts while perched on the back of a sofa, and over balanced.

If they had been having a dispute and Robert had given David a rough time, David could always find a way to get his own back. David would hide Robert's pens and pencils, or something he would need for school, just to wind him up at the last minute. One day I gave David two biscuits; one for him and one to take out to Robert. I watched with interest as David ate one and half of the other, before giving Robert the remaining half. Robert thought David was generously sharing his treat so they were both happy. There were times when it was better for me to keep quiet.

One dark winter's night, when a storm was raging and the wind was howling and whistling through all the cracks and crevices in the old house, I went up to check that the boys were ok. Three of them were fast asleep but to my horror Ricky had disappeared. His bed was empty and he was nowhere to be seen. I looked all over the house and was beginning to panic. With my heart pounding, I went back upstairs to do another check. Robert woke and I was so relieved to find Ricky fast asleep, snuggled down under Robert's covers. The noise of the wind had frightened him so he had taken refuge with his big brother.

Robert, full of good ideas as always, thought it would be wise to have a fire drill, so he made his brothers jump out of the bedroom window and gave Ricky, only four years old, an umbrella to use as a parachute on the descent. As he came down, the umbrella turned inside out, but fortunately he landed safely if a little bruised. I did not learn about this escapade until some years later.

John loved making things. George's father used to bring him old pram wheels to play with and at six years old he made his first little buggy using the wheels with some planks of wood and a box.

George liked to eat moorhen eggs. We had quite a lot of moorhens nesting on our ponds. One day the boys had taken a couple of eggs from one of the nests and were bringing them home for George's breakfast when one started to hatch out on the way. They christened him Fred and he became a pet. Some mornings they had him pitter-pattering with his webbed feet over the breakfast table, sharing their breakfast.

Ricky was allowed to go off with his brothers and some of the local lads, as long as someone sensible kept an eye on him. One day he came home wearing a huge, thick, blue pullover which reached down to his ankles. Butch, one of the older local lads had thoughtfully lent him the jumper and brought Ricky safely home. He mentioned that a little accident had occurred as he handed me a small pair of wet pants from his jacket pocket.

They had all learnt to drive the tractors at a very young age, which inspired David to buy his first car when he was just eight years old. He had thought that it would be a good idea to invest some of his hard earned money that he had saved up. He had seen a car advertised locally outside a house on the way to school, and managed to persuade Chris, one of George's friends, to take him to collect it. It was an old A30 and had belonged to a student who had left it parked, blocking his parents' driveway, while he had gone travelling abroad. It was in their way and they were happy to see the back of it, and after a little bartering, sold it to David for the grand sum of £5. After buying it, David did very well financially as he charged his brothers every time they drove it up and down the drive. One winter when the drive was covered in ice, David said that he thought it would be better if he drove my car down to the main road for me as he had more experience, having practised on a skid track in the field. He used to drive his car to the farm entrance, then walk to the garage in Kingsfold and the owner, who was known as Uncle Rusty, would fill his cans up with petrol for him. One day John had an accident on his motorbike and David used his little car as an ambulance when he and Ricky went to John's rescue. They picked him up and threw him in the car, drove him back and brought him to the kitchen with one carrying his legs and the other carrying his head. They laid a rather battered John on the kitchen floor, but fortunately he had suffered no major injuries, which is more than could be said for the motorbike.

When the boys were older they were allowed to roll the fields, which meant they had to drive the tractor very slowly up and down to flatten the ground that the cows had poached in the wet weather. George went out to discover that Robert had been speeding up and down, obviously having great fun, but he had gone through a fence into the wood, unable to stop in time.

John had discovered that if he wrapped a few match-heads in foil and put them under the Aga top, once they became hot they exploded. John and his best friend took this further. They put live matches in a tube in the vice in the workshop and fired nails at a target when they lit the matches. These escapades did not come to light until later when there was a sudden shortage of matches in the house.

One evening Robert thought they would play darts in the old dairy and lit a Tilly lamp. He could not find any paraffin to keep it going, so used diesel oil instead. The game did not last long before they were smoked out.

Ricky had a friend who came to play on one freezing cold winter morning. I told him that on no account were they to attempt to walk over a plank, which served as a bridge over the pond to the island. Ricky's friend thought that if he crossed the bridge on a trike, that wouldn't be walking over, thus complying with my instructions. Inevitably he fell in fully clothed, but fortunately lived to tell the tale.

One summer day one of the hovels mysteriously caught fire and the fire engine was called. It came with a full crew of firemen who put out the blaze. Years later it emerged that the fire had been caused by an "experiment", but to this day I have never found out anything more than that the experiment "got a little out of hand".

When the conker season came round, David stowed his away in a drawer in the bedroom. Before the house had central heating most of their clothes were kept downstairs in the kitchen where it was warm and dry. One morning when the conker season was over, I opened the drawer and found that a family of mice had taken up residence.

John, with his usual fascination for making things, welded two bikes together to make a tandem, on which they all had fun. However he was always fed up with his brothers pinching his lunchtime biscuits, so solved that problem by fixing a large padlock on his biscuit tin!

Robert, full as ever of bright ideas, wondered how long it would take to boil a puddle. He thought a blow lamp he was using had gone out, so poured some more methylated spirit on. The lamp flared up in his face and fortunately did no more damage than singe his eyebrows. First aid was applied and it wasn't long before his eyebrows grew back.

All the boys had their pets. Robert had his gundog, Jane and a few ducks. John kept pigeons and also a little kid from Lucky the goat. John would let it walk up and down on the keys of an old piano that stood in a shelter outside the stables, which it seemed to think was fun. Sadly the little kid met its death in an encounter with the greyhounds. David had three piglets to rear on for meat, and was very upset when he only received half price for the tiny runt of the litter.

Ricky had Paddy, a cheeky pony from Ireland. They made a good pair and when Ricky was old enough they went off to pony camp. Later when he was in his early teens, he used to jump up on an unbroken thoroughbred filly and ride her bareback. She would charge wildly around the field and he would jump off when they were at the nearest point to the house, which saved him walking from the bottom of the field. He also dared to ride Fred, the large Hereford bull, but only once!

One day when shooters had killed some squirrels, the boys rescued their two little babies and brought them home. They were lively little pets and became very tame, so much so that one day when George sought refuge in the old sitting room to read his paper, the two leaped on to his chair having jumped down from the curtains. It rather disturbed a tranquil moment. The boys had forgotten to put them back in their cage. It was not unknown for the squirrels to be vaulting around the bedroom at bedtime. They began to become more aggressive as they matured and with a young child in the flat, they were a liability. We took them to Chessington Zoo, a deed for which I have never been forgiven, because the boys were never sure whether they were given the happy home we hoped, or served to another animal for dinner. They were certainly nowhere to be seen on our next visit.

When John was around twelve years old, I started to keep bees. Robert made one of my hives in his woodwork class at school and we all became fascinated in the life of a bee. We attended classes and demonstrations. Two ladies from a bee keeping group came to help us set up and another man called in now and again with interesting tips and advice, passing on his knowledge. He kept bees commercially for honey and pollination, moving them to various areas.

A whole new world began to unfold when my Father made an observation hive. John set it up in his bedroom and apart from the odd bee that forgot to enter the hive through the specially inserted tube in the window pane and came in through the open window and buzzed around the bedroom, we could watch them working and realised what amazing little creatures they are.

I used to sit on the end of the bed and watch in awe as the worker bees came in laden with pollen and nectar and did their famous waggle dance to inform the others about to go out foraging in which direction the best and nearest pollen could be found; perhaps a field of clover or rape. With the help of the hive and the talks and demonstrations I enjoyed, I discovered the secrets of a bee colony's cycle.

Once some nurse and worker bees have been introduced to the hive they feed a few cells with special royal jelly to make queens. The first one to hatch kills the others so she remains head of the hive. Later she mates with up to twenty drones, which die after mating or are killed off in the autumn as they are not needed in the hive over winter. For every queen bee there can be up to 40,000 or so workers and nurse bees. The queen can live up to five years but will usually take some of the hive away to new surroundings by swarming. The workers only live for around 40 or so days and will forage up to five miles from the hive.

Extracting honey from our hives in the autumn was rewarding, delicious and well worth a few stings. We never robbed them of all their honey and always supplemented them with enough to help them through the winter months.

I have recently read the latest discovery about bees is that they are being trained to detect narcotics and explosives and can also help with some medical diagnoses.

HARMONY

Oh, have you seen the beauty
in the hedgerow down the lane.
The honey bees on duty,
after showers of Summer rain.
An awe inspiring spectre,
each one a job to do,
They forage for their nectar,
just think, it's quite like you.

Each day from dawn till dusk you toil,
Life can be very tough,
The rising costs, the price of oil.
Sometimes you've had enough.
So stop, and look and listen,
and ponder for a while.
The sun like gold will glisten,
and soon, you too will smile.

As you gaze into the hedgerow,
and you think of many things,
how plants can cope with frost and snow,
the way birds control their wings.
Look around, see, hear, take heart.
Forget those sorrows and all strife.
Just search your soul. Play a part,
in nature's Orchestra of Life.

Written in an hour one evening after a happy walk with the dogs,
feeling contented and peaceful with the world.

It was always time to be extra vigilant when children from the village
came to play. On one of these occasions I went out to investigate, and
found them clustered round the large circular saw. They had taken the
heavy piece of rubber tyre off the sharp blade that was normally driven by
a belt from the tractor, and were pawing the pully round with their hands
in an effort to work the blade to saw a piece of wood. It was a long time
before they ventured back to play on the farm again!

Robert went on to The Forest Boys School in Horsham and to his joy they did chemistry. He thought he would introduce his brothers to this wonderful subject. I was horrified when I found them standing in a line, well back from the old Calor Gas Cooker in the utility room, while he demonstrated to them just how much gas you needed to blow the top off a tin. Although Robert was studious, the others were not very interested in school. It later came to light that they all, except Robert, suffered from dyslexia. It seemed to have been inherited from the family of George's Mother. George himself, like the three boys, had struggled with reading and spelling but all were compensated by being very creative and practical, having a natural talent for many things that other people found difficult.

CHAPTER 17

Family Life

In 1968, once all the boys were going to school, I decided that it would be a good idea to set foot out into the big wide world again. Although I already had a motorbike licence, now was the time to learn to drive a car. With the money I was making from the greyhounds I could afford to take driving lessons, so I found a good local driving instructor, a middle aged Scotsman. As well as teaching me to drive, during my lessons he brought me up to date with many of the latest local goings on and offered me much useful advice on how to deal with people.

I was thrilled when I passed my driving test and was free to take to the road – if and when I could borrow George's car. I will never forget my first foray, driving out of the end of the farm drive, with the cowman's wife Valerie for support. I felt absolutely exhilarated; free at last! Soon afterwards I bought my first car, a rather antiquated Morris Estate, which served its purpose well.

At about this time the elderly headmaster at Warnham School retired and a new head took over. He arrived with very modern ideas, and the school rocketed from about 25 years behind the times to almost 25 years ahead. Metric measurement was about to be introduced and there were big changes. The new Head called a meeting of the staff and parents. It was decided to form a Parent Teachers Association.

Once I had wheels and independence, I was able to attend the meetings and was flattered to be asked to join the committee, which I happily accepted, apparently because I was considered to have a flexible personality. I enthusiastically agreed to help the pupils with cycling proficiency training, which I did for several years all the time I had children in attendance at school.

Plans for the new Warnham School were being drawn up. Becoming involved in the village was interesting and certainly provided new elements to my life, and the boys' lives too. Robert was able to join the Cubs, and he would enjoy going to a friend's house in the village for tea before the Cub meeting and being brought home at the end of the session. David sang in the Church choir and the Vicar used to bring him home from practice. Ricky was lucky enough to attend the new Nursery school that had opened in the village when he was four, before joining the Infants school at five.

John was in his element when he was in the first class. He excelled in fixing all the little building bricks together and other practical games, but when it came to reading and writing he didn't want to know. His teacher told me "he has all his chairs up to the table, but had no intention of using them". I thought that it was a cruel and unjustified statement. She had not heard of and did not believe in dyslexia, which three of the four boys had to cope with. Although a handicap whilst they were young and at school, later in life their creative talents most certainly came to the fore.

Robert left the Junior school just before the change to the more modern ideas. He went to the Forest Boys School and settled in quite well. David meanwhile was caught up in the middle of the modernisation upheaval and was taught by about ten different supply teachers, one of whom he did not see eye to eye with. I was summoned to the school to see her. While I listened to her side of the story, David stood between us. Imagine my embarrassment when he turned to me and said "There you are, I told you she was an old cow"! For a moment I wished the earth would open up and swallow me, although I have to admit I was inclined to agree with him. I made him apologise profusely and I said how sorry I was for his outrageous behavior. She accepted the apologies but had left the School within the month. David later went on to The Holy Trinity School on the outskirts of Crawley, which was a newly built comprehensive school unveiled by the Queen.

Around the time John started at Holy Trinity, I was taken very ill with a meningococcal virus. The headache was horrendous and I couldn't bear the light. I will always remember watching John trying to pack a case for me, as I waited in my bed for an ambulance to take me to hospital. He held a nightdress up and waved it backwards and forwards, to and fro, until it had fitted itself into the case. I looked over to Leith Hill in the distance in a semi-conscious haze as the ambulance doors closed on me, wondering if I would ever see the beautiful view again. George actually had a tear in his eye, so I knew things were extremely serious. In the hospital I was kept in a darkened room and given a lumbar puncture. The virus was identified and believed to have been carried by rats. I was out of action for nine weeks, and while recuperating I remember patching the boys' jeans that had holes in the knees – I think about twenty pairs!

We had a cowman who used a swear word in almost every sentence. When the boys tried to copy him and continued to do so in conversation, they had a bar of carbolic soap put into their mouth. It rubbed against their teeth as they bit it, which had a lasting effect. They soon found a better way to express themselves. The same cowman was going through a traumatic time as his wife had just left him, having absconded with his brother. I looked after their two boys, who were much the same age as mine, they were all used to playing together. I had them until their aunts and uncles came to the rescue. It was a very distressing time for them.

We once offered two young children from London a two week holiday on the farm. They were incredibly streetwise and told me they had been warned never to accept money or gifts from any man if he asked them to hold his willy! They were lovely youngsters and enjoyed their holiday with no disastrous mishaps.

The first time that George's daughters Mary and Sheila came to stay, they were just in their teens. I took them for a walk to show them the greyhounds. We came back round a corner beside the house and there, in full view, were two naughty little boys seeing how far they could pee into the garden from their upstairs bedroom window! It was always fun when the girls came to stay; they kept the boys amused and all got on very well.

When Ricky was about eight, I received a phone call from his headmaster, who by then I knew quite well. I was absolutely shocked when he tactfully asked me if I realised that Ricky was in possession of some pornographic magazines which he was trying to sell for a penny each. I had no idea where they came from and was lost for words. On closer investigation, we discovered that a couple of George's friends, who had been renting the flat in the farmhouse for a while before taking over the local pub, had left behind stacks of old newspapers and magazines which were piled up high in a cupboard. The boys had been given the task of clearing them all out and David, who was always careful never to throw anything valuable away, had found the offending magazines amongst the pile of newspapers. He had sorted them out and was selling them to some of the older boys at his school. Ricky had been given some to keep him quiet, and to teach him a lesson in improving his finances, revealing the touch of business acumen that David has possessed, and progressed, from an early age.

The Head of Warnham School, along with the staff, were keen to build a swimming pool so it was decided to organise a fete to help raise the required funds. There was much careful planning, and I was playfully goaded into agreeing to become a fortune teller for the day. A caravan was provided and I made my own preparations so that I could present myself as authentically as possible. I read a book all about fortune telling and went with a friend to see a gypsy lady in a rather seedy part of London to have my fortune told, just to see how it was done and to make sure I could adopt the correct patter. I went to Brighton Pier for another session to make sure I hadn't missed anything, and felt armed with plenty of know-how when the big day of the fete arrived. I took up residence in the caravan, and dressed for the occasion, became Gypsy Rosy Knees for the afternoon! The fete was a great success with all the stalls making a good profit, and the school was able to purchase and install a swimming pool for the children.

By this time I was earning money from my breeding and keeping greyhounds, and with my new found wealth I was able to pay for Robert to have extra maths lessons. David went to a piano teacher because he was quite musical and keen to play and Ricky and John went off to a local riding school for lessons.

We used to visit my old Headmaster Mr Gould and his wife on Sundays. Mrs Gould would help John with the reading and writing that he found so difficult. It was a great help, I used to do what I could to help him with his homework, which usually involved bribing him with jam tarts to encourage him along the way. Mrs Gould loved her garden and always gave us a tour to view her prize plants when she had finished working with John. Mr Gould took John up to London to show him the big city and took the time to explain interesting facts to him. One day he told John that when speaking to somebody who had been drinking a lot

My Grandfather
– My mother's father.

My Dad.

My Mum.

Grandparents
Left to right: Father's Father,
Mother's Father, Mother's Mother
and Father's Swiss Mother.

Dad, first speed cop in Surrey
Red Wing Panther, 1920s.

Brenda at 6 years old.

Yvonne my sister and me in front of our house, 20 Hilltop Road, Reigate.

Me with kid at Sheephatch,
aged 14 years.

Me with Sandra eating my hair,
aged 15 years.

A day at the sea,
aged 17 years.

Back of OldWattlehurst Farmhouse, Sussex stone roof.

Side of the house with part built on in the late 1800s.

The Old Copper House where I did the washing, complete with a well, 16th century.

Built in the 16th Century. Old Wattlehurst Side of the house.

Robert meeting my mum and dad for the first time, 1957.

George and me in Jersey first short break, 1959.

Dressed ready for the Greyhound Awards night in London, 1970s.

At home under the damson tree.

Jo and me with Uncle Fitz the day he brought my parents down. Re-united after 2 years, 1957.

*Robert offering Joe
a cup of milk, 1959.*

Lucky and Joe, 1959.

*David in the tub after
playing with a tin of green
paint. The cat stepping over
the wet paint patches, 1961.*

George with Mum and Dad,
late 1950s.

Mary, Me, David, Sheila,
John and Robert, 1962.

A day at the sea
Robert, George with John,
David and Neil, 1962.

John, Robert, Joe and David 1962

John, David, Mary and Robert, 1962.

Ricky with Robert, David and John, 1963.

Robert with Ricky, John and David in a cornfield, 1963.

Robert at milking time, 1963.

David, Ricky, Robert and John with Jenny at milking time, 1963.

Milking time, 1963.

Me with youngsters, 1961.

Greyhounds and Joe, 1965.

George disciplining
greyhounds, 1965.

Me putting on leads after racing
round the field, 1965.

Robert and David with
Joe and pups, 1961.

Relaxing in the yard, 1962.

Poppet, John and Joe, 1960

Misty with David, Ricky and John in the front garden, 1964.

Ricky on Gypsy and Jane, 1968

David, John, Robert and Ricky, 1967

Rough but ready. Robert, John and David and Ricky, 1968

John, Robert and David just home from school, 1968

Ricky, John, David and Robert just off to school, 1965.

Me, David, Ricky and John having a day out in the New Forest, 1969

of alcohol, you might just as well talk to the bottle. I know now that they realised that all was not well in that direction with George at home, and with hindsight it is a pity I had not taken any notice of this sound advice.

At mealtimes Robert and Ricky were ordered to sit next to George at the table as they were the naughtiest. They were then within reach of a cuff around the ear when they misbehaved. George would often say "Manners cost nothing", only with the next breath to shout "Salt!" or demand that something be fetched for him from the cupboard without as much as a please or a thank you. One day when just home from the pub, George told Ricky to "Sit up and eat your tea". Ricky replied cheekily "I can't eat my tea, I drink it", for which he would have received a smart clout if he hadn't ducked to miss and ran out of the kitchen. George chased in hot pursuit, brandishing a chair which unfortunately bashed into the fridge as he went to dive through the door. A large dent in the fridge remained as a reminder of the episode for many years. When Ricky was safely outside, he dared to come back to the open kitchen window and stuck his tongue out, put his thumbs in his ears and waggled his fingers at his father, before running off. He returned much later, confidently knowing that after George had slept a while his father would have no recollection of the incident.

Remembering my driving instructor's advice to push hard for things that I believed in and not to take no for an answer, I started to look around at Boarding Schools. I was not too happy with thirteen year old Robert's cocky behaviour. He was ready to spread his wings and I believed that a change of environment for him would be a good thing. It was time to do a little pruning.

Unfortunately, George was not the type of role model I had envisaged or desired for the boys. He was spending more and more time at the pub drinking, and a Jekyll and Hyde character was beginning to emerge. The boys later christened his state of mood as the "dipstick effect", as he would change depending on how much liquor had been consumed. The George we knew would walk out of the door, but more and more often a complete monster would crash through the door on his return home. He was also gambling heavily, and was very tight with money for everyday essentials. I had to survive on the £6 a week he gave me for housekeeping. Luckily milk, eggs and vegetables were available from the farm. The boys were made to load up manure into sacks and saw logs, both of which were taken down to the end of the drive for people to buy. Money was left in an honesty box, which went straight into George's pocket as beer money. On Sunday mornings when the milk levels were never tested at the dairy, George would put a little water into each churn to help pay for his whisky.

George expected the boys to work hard on the farm, and I did not have a problem with this, but there were limits. I knew they needed time to do their homework, but George sadly appeared to have little or no interest in their academic education. Having known him for nearly twenty years, I realised that he was not likely to change his mind on the issue.

I began to put out some feelers and found some good schools for children whose parents were working abroad. The Thomas Peacock Grammar School in Rye in East Sussex had just been made into one of the new Comprehensives and still had its Grammar School staff. It had a boarding facility called Leasam House, complete with a farm. It was just what I was looking for. Taking the bit between my teeth, I pulled a few strings to get Robert in.

I took advice from the Vicar, who knew that George had something of a reputation in the village. He suggested that I should measure whether the good times outnumbered the bad times or vice versa. He also told me that all the time I was not married to George, I had full control of the boys until they were sixteen. My Doctor also helped; he had seen me with the odd black eye, bruises and bashed ribs which, I hasten to add, I probably would not have sustained had I managed to keep quiet and not provoke George when he had been drinking. Nevertheless, with their help Robert, much to his disgust, was offered a place at Leasam House School.

Soon after Robert started in Rye, when I was driving him back after a half-term holiday, we were almost at our destination on a country road when a car shot out of a side road and hit us head on. We were fortunate that the first person to arrive at the scene of the accident was an ambulance driver who was just going to start his shift. We were all quite shaken, and he was very helpful and took control of the situation until the Police and an ambulance arrived. David managed to pick up a piece of the car with the name badge on as a souvenir before we were taken off to hospital for a checkup. Robert had been very sensible, although shaken, and went straight on back to school. David, John, Ricky and I were given the all clear, except for a little bit of whiplash, and we went home by taxi. My car was written off by the insurance company, and the other driver was later prosecuted for dangerous driving.

It was strange how without Robert at home the peck order changed. All went well until the holidays, when all four were back together again. It took about a week for them to sort it out, after which order was restored with Robert back on top. I found myself comparing them with the greyhounds, as they too have a way of vying for position, and there always has to be a top dog, and as the eldest it had always been Robert. However at Leasam it was a very different story. Robert had to start at the bottom and respect the older boys. Just like in Tom Brown's School Days, fagging still went on and Robert had to learn his lowly place. One day one of the older boys pinched some sodium from the Science Lab, and a group of them made Robert carry it to a field well away from the house, and ordered him to throw it in to a trough, then run. He had no idea what would happen. He threw it in the water as instructed, but turned to see what was happening. As it blew up, a spark went into his eye. The bullies took him back to the house and washed his eye out, and told him to say that some Jeyes fluid had splashed in his eye. He was in agony. The next day, one of the teachers was suspicious of the story and whisked him off to Hastings Hospital where the truth came out. A girl who was in the same class as Robert phoned her mother, who lived not far from Wattlehurst, and told her what had happened. The mother then phoned me to see if I had been told, which of course I had not. I was very grateful to her and realised that the incident had been kept from me until the outcome was certain. Fortunately Robert's eye made a full recovery. I wrote to the Headmaster demanding a full explanation, and received a very apologetic reply. As it happened, it was a blessing in disguise as Robert was elevated into the Science Stream after the incident and never really looked back.

It had been a good decision to send Robert to Leasam House; he participated in the school plays, played rugby, learned the skill of public speaking and had a Biology master who gave him the encouragement he needed to catch up to a Grammar school level. He later became Head Boy and passed his A-levels before he left. He went into the Police Cadets for a while, and then went on to work in pharmaceutical research. When he was old enough he joined the Sussex Police and became a traffic officer, following in my Father's footsteps; they both had a passion for motorbikes. He later left the Police force to start a Plant Nursery where his knowledge of biology came to the fore. He was always interested in politics and later became Leader of the Local Council.

David too went to Leasam House at thirteen, and left school at sixteen with no qualifications. It was good for him to experience life away from home at a mixed school. He seemed to fit in and was no trouble.

When he left school, he worked for a year on the farm before he bought a lorry and started up a removal business and later an express transport company, working here and overseas. He finally started a Builders Merchant company but always kept a keen interest in owning and racing cars, winning championship races in Seat and Ford cars.

John and Ricky went on to the Holy Trinity School. John stayed there until he left. Farming was in his blood and he wanted to do nothing else. He left school as soon as he could at sixteen and worked for a year on the farm, attending Brinsbury Agricultural College a couple of days a week. He then went on a residential course at Merrist Wood, the Surrey Agricultural College, for a year and came out with flying colours. He then took over the running of the dairy herd at home. Shortly before his 21st birthday he had a horrendous accident, but fortunately made a miraculous recovery. Much later he moved to France and single handedly transformed a rundown old French farmhouse and adapted barns and paddocks to accommodate thoroughbred broodmares and young stock for racing and set up facilities for a herd of Charolais cattle and Dorset sheep.

Ricky left his mark on Holy Trinity School. One winter's day when it had been snowing hard, the school closed early so the students could get home before the roads became impassable. Unfortunately the school bus kept to its usual time so the youngsters were left outside for quite a while before it arrived. They were having a fine time hurling snowballs at one another, and unfortunately a stray one hit the windscreen of a car belonging to a young student master. Thinking it was Ricky who had thrown the offending snowball, the master sent him to the Headmaster. Ricky was then nearly sixteen years old and was incensed at being accused of something he had not done. He decided to take the law into his own hands, and grabbing the young master by the lapels he called him a "snivelling little pipsqueak". Ricky was suspended from school and the head asked to see us. George refused to go, so Robert, who was then in the Police Force, came with me and it was agreed that if Ricky apologised he could continue his studies. The head was very amicable and commented that he felt school was not for Ricky, but that whatever he decided to do in the future, he would do well. This was encouraging to hear and turned out to be very true.

Ricky left school at the earliest opportunity. At the Leavers' Party he climbed up a drainpipe and on to the roof of the science block to retrieve a football that someone had kicked up there. He thought it would be a good idea to see the view from higher up, so throwing the ball down he continued to climb up to the third storey. Having admired the view, he decided he would take a short cut back down, so jumped down to the second storey which had a flat roof. As he landed unfortunately his foot went right through the roof into the staff room. The bill for the damage came to £700. Ricky went on to work very hard on the farm for a year to pay it all off, earning just £60 a month.

CHAPTER 18

The Horse Era

Once the children were old enough and we had become established at Wattlehurst, George and I agreed that it would be good for the children to have a pony. George bought Poppet, a grey filly. She was well behaved but although Robert was able to ride her, she was too big and began to grow an ever expanding girth from too much good food and not enough exercise. She needed to be with someone who could spend more time with her and take her to gymkhanas and shows. Fortunately we found a lovely home for her with friends with little girls who idolised her.

Next came Jeffrey, a 14 hand bay pony who George acquired from a deal he had done with a diddicoy at the pub. Jeffrey seemed quiet enough when he first arrived, having been ridden all the way over from Dunsfold, which was about 20 miles away. However, a day or two later, once he had recovered, his behaviour changed rapidly. On closer examination we discovered that he was a rig, which means he had an un-descended testicle producing an odd and unpredictable temperament. Jeffrey didn't stay long: he was too much of a liability.

Paddy came next, a 14 hand, skewbald gelding from Ireland. John and Ricky used to ride him. David was allergic to horse scurf, so didn't over indulge in horse riding but stuck to his car, preferring four wheels to four hoofs. Ricky went pony clubbing with Paddy – he was a very wily pony. One day I watched him escape from his paddock. He cleverly stepped sideways through the post and rail fence. I couldn't believe my eyes and I've never seen another do it from that day to this.

Later we had Gypsy, a little piebald pony and Sugar, a little chestnut, both loved by all, including, later, the grandchildren.

In the early 1970s, George bought his first thoroughbred brood mare, a 16 hand bay named Bella Lisa. This for me was when the real "horse era" began, and was to become a lifetime passion.

Thunderbolt

George he was a farmer,
stubborn, sturdy and strong.
Lord and heaven help yer,
should you do he a wrong!

He did buy a blood horse,
all broken down was she.
Abuse'd on the race course,
and she was not yet three.

George he had an eye for stock,
the mare was no exception.
True she'd had a nasty knock,
but that was a deception.

Being fed upon the best,
she thrived; George called her Kate.
When she'd had a good long rest
he soon found her a mate.

A stallion mighty of great fame
fathered the babe; a colt.
George gave yon little foal a name,
'Twas christened Thunderbolt.

Nurtured well, the colt it grew
on milk, grass, hay and jollop.
The latter George's special brew
fed by administering a dollop.

His methods not quite orthodox,
though he rode him mouthed with bit.
Strange methods did our George concoct,
and eventually both were fit.

Muscles were all a quiver
the day of that great race,
George gave a little shiver,
he hoped they'd hold the pace.

Well, he pulverised the track
on yon plucky, pounding colt.
George riveted to his back,
won six lengths with Thunderbolt.

Fame and fortune George had found.
Kate's effort, he'd not dismiss
Late that night I'll be bound,
George came home Brahms and Liszt!

Written in 1982, inspired by George's first racehorse Bella Lisa.

The origin of the thoroughbred horse is an intriguing story dating back to the 1680s, at the time when The Ottoman Empire was a powerful presence in eastern Europe. At The Battle of The Boyne, a Captain Byerley captured a magnificent Turkish stallion, which he named Byerly Turk. He became the foundation stallion and all thoroughbreds can be traced back to him. His blood was crossed with an Arab horse called Darley Arabian from Syria and Godophin Arabian from the Yemen and many years later American quarter horse blood was bred in introducing and producing the more speedy sprinter, as opposed to what is known as the steeplechaser. Landowners used to race steeplechasers across their fields, jumping over hedges and ditches, to see who could find the quickest route from one village church steeple to the next. These developed into today's Grand National types of thoroughbred, usually big, strong, rangy horses that can jump well. Warm bloods are other well known breeds, with a dash of thoroughbred blood blended in to give them a classy look and conformation along with a lively spark.

George's newly acquired mare had been racing and had shown great promise until her career was cut short when she went lame and she was pensioned off to become a brood mare. She later produced several winners, the first one being a colt christened Kingsfold Trooper by George. He won several good races before George sold him. With the proceeds of his wins the leaking farmhouse roof was completely re-tiled.

Lisa's next foal was Kingsfold Lad, who sadly broke a leg and had to be put down.

She produced several more foals, including a filly who won The Rippolin Paint Stakes at Goodwood. This gave us the opportunity to meet the Lord and Lady who owned the Goodwood House Estate. I was invited back to the big house to take afternoon tea with the charming Lady, while George went off chatting about paint with the Lord, who, to our embarrassment, George thought was just someone from the Rippolin Paint firm!

With the knowledge that I had gained from breeding the racing greyhounds and having been blessed with so many exciting winners, I became fascinated by blood lines, especially the hereditary factors versus rearing ones. With racing dogs, there are so many ways the dice can fall – a litter provides so many variables. There is an old saying: "A little bit bred in, a little bit fed in, and a hell of a lot of luck."

Twenty years and many litters later, I was very tempted to try out the same breeding theories with race horses, but with four growing sons, finances were somewhat strained.

When Charlie, one of the owners I was rearing puppies for, asked if I would like to buy a good thoroughbred brood mare, I was very keen, but knew that I could not really afford her. Charlie was a real character who could almost have kidded a duck to carry an umbrella. His father was a horse dealer, who had supplied the local dairies with horses to pull the milk delivery carts. Charlie had an eye for a good horse, although he found dealing in scrap metal and property equally lucrative and it enabled him to cruise round in a beautiful Rolls Royce car, which had the most sumptuous interior, complete with thick, azure blue carpet to nestle your feet in. We used to go to the races with him sometimes and when we had horses to sell he would always enquire what the reserve price was, then keep the bidding going briskly from the start and back out once the reserve price had been reached.

Each Sunday when he came to see his puppy we would haggle over the price of the mare, but to no avail. Then one day I offered to swop a promising young greyhound dog for her. He agreed and the deal went through. I proudly took possession of a rather temperamental animal who, although well bred and in foal, was a little difficult, with a voracious appetite for human flesh and quite handy with her heels too. The blacksmith did ask, with tongue in cheek, if she had belonged to a circus, as she threw herself to the ground and lay prostrate when he first attempted to trim her feet. Eventually she quietened down and produced a healthy foal.

In 1977, George and I went to the Newmarket Sales where he was looking to buy a filly foal to run as a companion for Bella Lisa's latest, newly weaned foal. For just five hundred pounds, he bought the cutest little chestnut filly. I loved her from the moment I first set eyes on her. She had such presence; I christened her Dolly Daydream. She looked so lost, having just been weaned and taken away from her mother back home in Wales and was very wary of all the hubbub at the sales, but once back home on the farm, she soon settled in and grew into a very cheeky little filly.

She eventually raced under the name of Kingsfold Flash. She was placed third then second and we were confidently expecting a good win at Epsom on Oaks Day when she succumbed to a virus infection which ended her racing career. Dolly was turned out to graze for the rest of the summer. With the sun on her back, she quickly recovered. I was devastated when George announced "She must go." So I sadly decided to sell the mare and foal that I had bartered for, and breed from Dolly instead, as she had both Flat Race and National Hunt blood running through her veins.

I paid George eight hundred pounds of my hard earned cash for her, then sat thumbing through the book of Sires, trying to find a suitable stallion at the right price. Swing Easy was my choice. He was a big, strong, well bred American stallion, good looking, reasonably priced and standing at stud not too far away.

The result of the covering was a big filly, who was later named Four Sport by new owners when I had sold her. She raced from three to seven years old and was then retired to stud having won and been placed in several good races each year.

For the next stallion I again searched the pages of the book of Sires, and was drawn to Great Nephew, a beautifully well balanced horse, with a wonderful pedigree that blended with Dolly's, but alas with a stud fee way out of my bracket. At the back of the book the cheaper stallions were advertised and I came across an almost unknown one named No Loiterer. He was out of a famous Hyperion mare by my favoured Great Nephew, and had run ninety-six races and finished sound, with a large percentage of wins and places over both the flat and jumps. He was a half brother to five other good winners too, one a well known classic winner named Frankincense, who had been snapped up and exported to Japan for stud duties. No Loiterer was mainly just covering event horses, but from the three pure thoroughbreds he had sired, he had produced one winner and two placed horses. When I phoned to enquire about him, a little boy (who by chance later became a top jockey) answered the phone with a broad Midlands accent. He assured me that the horse had "loovely legs" and was quiet enough for him to ride. I was intrigued and interested enough to travel up to the midlands to view the "loovely legs." I was very impressed as he looked so like Hyperion, the great broodmare sire, whose famous offspring had captured the hearts of the racing fraternity twenty years previously. No Loiterer's stud fee was just one hundred and fifty pounds, plus fifty pounds for the groom. I also obtained a sincere promise that they would look after Dolly and her Swing Easy foal, still at foot, for the time that they were at the stud. I decided that No Loiterer was just the right stallion for Dolly. He had excellent conformation and his bloodlines would blend well with hers, doubling up on the Hyperion line. With luck, strong recessive genes remain dominant and pass on the desired traits.

The following year on Derby Day, Kingsfold Flame was born. She grew into a very classy looking little filly, chestnut and peacocky like her mother. I had taken a lot of criticism for putting the mare to an unknown stallion but to me, somehow, it always felt right. I sent Flame back up to the No Loiterer stud in Rutland to be broken and schooled. They were experts and knew the old stallion's progeny well.

I was advised to hold Flame back until she was aged three before racing her, at which time I had her re-schooled in an indoor school before she went into training with Mick Haynes, who I knew treated all his horses as individuals. It was an expensive occupation; I worked hard and sold at car boot sales to help pay for all her schooling. The hard work and the gamble paid off; I leased her to George and his friends to race for three seasons. She beat colts almost twice her size which had been bred from astronomically expensive stock. Flame's claim to fame was when she ran in England, Ireland, France and Belgium, one mile to a mile and a quarter on the flat, winning ten heart-stopping races, and being placed eight times. Her winnings came to almost ninety thousand pounds.

One of her most memorable races was when George had gone to Lingfield, as he had one of his horses racing there, and I went up to York with Mike, the trainer.

The sky darkened and storm clouds brewed as the horses came out on parade before the big race. They were on their toes, uneasy with the strange sultry atmosphere, when suddenly, a huge flash of lightening, then a mighty crash of thunder sent the horses and their handlers scurrying back to the saddling boxes for shelter. Flame came out after the storm and pranced around the paddock. She was the smallest filly in the race, dwarfed by her expensive male rivals. It was breathtaking to watch her slowly make her way through the field, brilliantly ridden, to just pip the favourite at the post. I proudly led her in and was interviewed on television. Aside the obvious proud memories of the day, I also remember clearly thinking afterwards that for the first time in my life I'd had soaking wet feet and never felt them squelching!

The most exciting of the racing escapades was when Robert, who by then had a pilot's licence, flew George and his friends to Brussels for another of Flame's races. It was a £20,000 group one race. Mike, the trainer and I went by boat. We both felt happier on the sea. Just before the race, a horse cast a shoe and the race was held up while a farrier replaced it. Many of the horses became restless but Flame remained reasonably calm. After another heart-fluttering experience, Flame won. As the breeder, I received a beautiful trophy of a bronze horse. George and his syndicate split the prize money. Celebrations were in full swing when Robert became concerned about the weather. The wind had started to blow a gale and storm clouds were scudding across the sky. Robert was piloting a small hired plane from Shoreham and he wanted to make a move. Mike and I left to catch the ferry. While we were crossing, the gale struck and the sea became very rough. We made it safely to the other side. The plane however, was diverted to come in further over towards the east coast. George and his syndicate had lingered too long. Having celebrated their winnings, they had drunk a few more drams than nature had capacity for, which caused an embarrassing situation in the small plane.

When Flame ran a race in Ireland, we went over in a small chartered plane. She came third. The jockey who was Irish, made the most of his trip home to Ireland by joining his friends after the race which lead to him being late to meet us for the flight back. The light was fading when we reached the private airfield and car headlights had to light up the grass strip as the pilot brought us safely down to land. I am not a very confident flyer at the best of times and I found the experience very scary.

Flame's last race was in France. I took Ricky and his fiancée Lynne over as an engagement present. We flew to Paris and spent a few days enjoying the places of interest, culminating in Flame's race at Longchamp, where she came fourth in her final race before retiring from racing to become a broodmare.

Dolly's next covering stallion was Broadsword. It was his first season at stud, he had not yet let down and was still very fit from racing, but the framework was all there. He was a big, strong, stallion who again made a good American out-cross with dual purpose blood, and his fee was reasonable too.

A year later John helped Dolly to deliver a huge colt, nick-named Sabre. I spent the whole night in the stable with them when he was born. His legs were so long, they looked like stilts and he had difficulty standing for the first time. It is incredible how a mare can carry such a large, long legged baby cocooned inside and how, if all goes well, within around twenty minutes or so of birth, the foal is up and sucking. It is so imperative that a foal has a good feed of colostrum within the first six hours of birth, as it contains antibodies from the mare protecting against local bugs and diseases. Sabre soon learned how to co-ordinate his legs and quickly grew into a very handsome young colt. Unable to retain him and Flame, who I wanted to keep for breeding, I sadly parted with him at the Doncaster Sales. Fortunately, because he looked so good, The Elms Stud, where his father Broadsword stood, bought him back in from the sales and ran him on, giving him time to mature. He later burst into the headlines as a six year old.

It was such a thrill for me when I received a phone call from The Elms, telling me that Sabre, my extraordinary long legged foal, was now called Flashing Steel and had won his first race by twelve lengths in Ireland, beating eight other good winners, and been sold to the Irish Premier for £100,000. Altogether he won fifteen races: three National Hunt flat eight over fences and four steeplechases and was placed 10 times, winning a total of £176,374. I had sold him as a yearling for just £4,000. He achieved a fourth in the Cheltenham Gold Cup. His greatest accolade was winning The 1995 Irish Grand National carrying home the colours of former Premier Charles Haughey. It speaks volumes for his trainer, John Mulhern, who managed to keep Flashing Steel fit and sound throughout his long racing career.

John Mulhern also trained Kingsfold Flash's last big winner, Miltonfield. He was by Little Wolf, chosen because his Grandsire, once again, was Great Nephew. It made an interesting combination of blue blood lines at the right price. The dominant recessive genes surfaced again and he won five flat races, twice winning the Irish Cesarewitch, two National Hunt wins on the flat and two over hurdles, and was placed twenty times winning a total of £130,000. I had sold him as a youngster for just £6,000.

Another of Kingsfold Flash's winners was On the Sauce. He won eight over hurdles and was placed 15 times, winning £18,196. Wenslydale Willy won one National Hunt flat and one hurdle and placed twice. His total winnings were £4,502.

These many successes were a great tribute to a cheeky little mare who originally cost just £500, and Stud Fees which didn't exactly break the bank. The total winnings of all Kingsfold Flash's progeny was £430,305.

Sadly Flash is no longer with us, but her memory lingers on. I have managed to keep one filly from each generation as a broodmare, to sustain the dam line.

CHAPTER 19

Ups and Downs through the Teenage Years

In 1972 I had made enough money from breeding and rearing the greyhounds to take the boys away on holiday. We had enjoyed the occasional day at the sea and they had been away to stay with friends and relations, but it would be our first holiday together as a family. I had not had a holiday for nine years. When I mentioned to George that I was thinking of going to Portugal with the boys, I asked him if he would come too. At first he was not very keen. The idea of going on holiday with four teenagers did not sound like a holiday to him, but then he changed his mind and decided he would join us.

We had an enjoyable time. One afternoon we decided to cross over the border into Spain. We had not gone far before we were stopped by the police, and George was marched off. Not speaking the language, we were not sure why, however after a few agonising minutes, they returned with George and we discovered that the car we had hired was not insured for Spain, but at least we were able to have a quick look around before returning back across the border.

Another afternoon we decided to visit a famous mountain where, on a clear day, one was supposed to be able to see the bay from which Vasco da Gama set sail on his voyages.

Robert was driving having recently passed his driving test. He had been driving tractors from a very young age and was a confident driver. We ascended higher and higher – Robert carefully negotiated the narrow bends along the crumbling road. When we looked down from the side closest to the edge, there was a terrifying, sheer drop. We were soon up in the clouds and I began to think it was not such a good idea, and when we reached the car park near the summit, the anticipated view had completely disappeared. After a break, we made a very scary descent. Other aspects of the trip were much more enjoyable; we visited fascinating harbours, the markets were interesting and the prawns we ate were divine.

When the coach came to take us back to Faro Airport, George was still in the hotel bar. The coach had to wait for him. He finally emerged, but when he came on board he was very drunk. He was loud mouthed, saying the most outrageous things, and to crown it all, there was a delay at Faro Airport. It was humiliating and so embarrassing in front of all our fellow passengers. His behaviour rather dampened our first, and last, family holiday.

Once the boys were well into their teens, they all had an avid interest in fast cars and girlfriends. On one occasion David brought his girlfriend, whom he was trying to impress, home to lunch. I had cooked a large joint of juicy rump steak, and George, who usually carved the meat, was watching horse racing on TV in the sitting room. I asked John to carve it instead. He pulled the whole joint in front of him, and as he held the carving knife and fork erect, one each side of the joint, he announced jokingly, that the whole joint would do him very well. David was furious that John was showing off in front of his girlfriend and suddenly a fight broke out over the table. It soon became very heated. The girl-friend stood up, shouting "Violence will get you nowhere!"

I went to fetch George. In the meantime Ricky had arrived and bravely stood between his two bigger brothers, trying to keep them apart. George finally barged into the kitchen, annoyed at being disturbed, and thinking Ricky was the cause of the trouble gave him one almighty wallop. Ricky staggered back, somewhat confused as to why he had taken the rap. However, peace was finally restored and the steak was shared out amicably.

Although the boys did not always see eye to eye, once they were adults it was rare for their disagreements to erupt into violence. The only other time I can recall, was when they were a little younger. A difference of opinion had taken place at the top of the stairs on a day when I had friends in for coffee. Ricky was cheeky to David who gave him a whack. Ricky bumped all the way down the stairs and crashed through the door into the kitchen, which caused a bit of a stir in front of the startled visitors. Most of the time over the years, dominance had been achieved by respect for age and a few mighty thumps. Once they were grown up, boundaries were challenged verbally.

One Saturday evening, John, his friend Walter, and their girlfriends were driving home down the steep hill from Coldharbour, negotiating the very twisty bends on the narrow road. Their car skidded off the track down into a densely wooded area, before it ground to a halt against a tree. Fortunately no-one was seriously injured. I received a rather sheepish telephone call, asking if I would go to the rescue. The girls were quite shaken, but otherwise just a little bruised with a couple of minor cuts. At crack of dawn the next morning, the boys drove the tractor up to the scene of the accident and reclaimed the rather bent and buckled car, before anyone had spied it hidden in the undergrowth and reported it.

One evening Ricky was proudly at the wheel of his pride and joy, a newly sprayed MG sports car, driving home up Bashurst Hill. He was horrified, as he rounded a bend, to see a herd of stampeding bullocks looming up in front of his headlights. They had escaped from their field and were cavorting down the narrow road towards him. Alas, the first two, unable to stop, clambered over the bonnet of his most treasured possession. The bonnet was completely destroyed, damaged beyond repair. David went to the rescue on that occasion, and it was fortunate that neither Ricky nor the cattle suffered the same fate as the car.

One day when I was going to the slaughter house to collect meat for the dogs, I suddenly realised that I was being followed by a police car. After a while it overtook me, then flashed me signalling me to stop. I pulled into the side, wondering whatever I had done wrong when who should come strutting up to my car but Robert, with a big grin on his face. He was on duty in the area and thought it was a huge joke. My language was not very ladylike, but I was relieved.

When David first started his transport business, in the days before mobile phones, he was not keen on using an answerphone. He thought it was better for prospective customers to speak to a person, so at break-neck speed, I used to rush in from outside to answer the phone as quickly as possible. I would then ask them what they required and tried to sound very efficient making it appear that David had a fleet of lorries. I would ask if they wanted a truck, flat back, or a box lorry. He had just one of each – only the box lorry was reasonably new. The flat back had been an old army lorry. He had started his enterprise on next to nothing.

CHAPTER 20

Spreading Wings

Once I had my own car and the babysitting days were over, I felt that at last it was my turn to spread my wings and I was free to go out in the evenings. With the money I had coming in from my greyhound clients, I could now afford to attend evening classes. While George spent his evenings down at the pub, I decided it was time to catch up with the education I had missed due to the disruption of war time. Having been evacuated twice, I had attended seven very different schools in England, Scotland and Wales, and had been taught some subjects two or three times, while other important ones, not at all.

George's unsupportive comment to me was, "And where the hell do you think that's going to get you?" That made me all the more determined, and over the next twenty or so years, I took O-levels in English, Biology, Human Biology, Modern History, and Maths. I went on to do a two year A-level Psychology Course in Horsham and later an interesting Social Psychology course at Guildford University. Each term I tried something new. I studied Science and Modern Day Thinking, Comparative Religions, Assertiveness, Body Language, Art, Investing Money, Woodwork for Housewives and Pensioners, Car Maintenance, Chinese Cookery, First Aid, Philosophy, Antiques, Typing, Pottery, Creative Writing and Computer Classes when they first started to arrive on the scene! I can add to that list a Modelling course that was less successful – I didn't feel confident baring my varicose veins in a bathing suit!

It was so enjoyable socialising with people who had similar objectives and were keen, as I was, to acquire new knowledge and learn new skills. I met so many people at the courses and made many friends, it was a positive time for me to venture out and have a bit of a life away from the family and the farm.

George and I realised that we were beginning to drift apart so in 1974 we made the effort to take a holiday together and went to Alderney for a few days. It was good to relax on a peaceful little island where the sea is never far away, and we whiled away the hours exploring the coves.

One evening in the bar we were talking with two gentlemen who had sailed over to the island in a yacht owned by one of them. Apparently they were old school friends whose wives were not keen on sailing, and they often spent weekends sailing together to France and the Channel Islands. They invited us to join them, so we met them the next morning, and were taken by dinghy over to their yacht. George and I had never been on a luxurious, expensive yacht before. It was quite an experience. Once we had left the harbour, my heart sank as I saw George's eyes light up when some bottles of brandy were produced. I stuck to just one glass.

After we had been sailing for a while, we came across a small boat not far away from us that was in trouble, so George and the friend left in the inflatable dinghy to offer assistance. We were by then quite a way from the harbour, and I was left alone with the yacht's owner. He became very amorous, and I spent the next half an hour trying to defend my honour, as he groped and mauled me in his brandy fuelled state. My first thought was to box his ears, but that could have inflamed the situation. I did contemplate jumping overboard, but although I was quite a strong swimmer, I don't think I would have made it to the shore, so I had no choice but to keep calm and played him along as I knew there was no escape.

It seemed like an eternity before the other two returned, having sorted the other boat's engine problem out. I did not let on what had happened, and they must have thought that the high colour of my cheeks and my ruffled hair, were due to the sea breeze. That night in the bar, while the others were talking, the yacht owner pulled me to one side and apologised profusely for his behaviour. I accepted his apology and never set eyes on him again. On first impressions, he had appeared to be a pleasant, genuine gentleman but the brandy had revealed another aspect of his character.

It always astonished me how sometimes the most unlikely men turned out to be wolves in sheep's clothing. I had worked with many earthy types and had learned how to ignore their advances. In my earlier years at Wattlehurst, I had trouble with a man who came to mend a machine. One of the dogs would not stop barking at the stranger so I calmed the dog down and gave it a tit-bit. The man then, with a wicked glint in his eye, sidled up close and said, "If I barked loud enough would you give me a little bit?" When George came home, I told him. He just thought it was amusing, and said it was the sort of thing most men did. I realised then that he was one of them. I later discovered that when Spring was in the air the postman suffered from the same overdose of male hormones when he promised that, if I was interested, he would just jump on and off like a little sparrow. In those days women were expected to endure suggestive remarks and other innuendoes.

The baker went further when he asked me if I preferred a large white or a large brown! He had passed George's car at the pub and knew I was alone. Having not succeeded in getting my trousers down, he showed me what I was missing. I had never seen anything like it. He was hung like a donkey! Fortunately, once I could drive there was no need for our bread to be delivered as I then bought it from the supermarket.

It was a little different with a friend of George's, who came to service our electrical appliances. I can't deny it; I really was attracted to him. When he came in for a cup of tea, just setting eyes on him caused me to feel an electric spark! On one occasion, I remember him tweaking the bars of Billy the budgerigar's cage, telling him not to say a word. Billy the budgie instantly bobbed up and down on his perch and replied with his newly learned party piece, "Georgie Porgie Puddin' and Pie". I'm pleased to say that fortunately, Billy never let on what he had seen!

In 1977 Robert was engaged to be married and George thought that it was the right thing for us to do likewise. Having lived with him for 22 years, remembering very well how he had already broken his first marriage vows, living with his often embarrassing behaviour and knowing what he got up to when he had been drinking, I was not overly keen. I felt things were better left as they were. It had never been a secret that we were not married. Nevertheless for legal reasons it made sense, so I said "Yes."

On April 18th 1977, we were married at Epsom Registry Office. Two secretaries witnessed the ceremony. I already had a ring but seldom wore it, because when handling stock there was the possibility that it could get caught and tear or break a finger. One morning, while I was making the beds, John, who was just a toddler, had managed to climb up and take the ring off the dressing table and put it on his finger. It transpired that he had worn it outside. When asked where it was, he pointed down a drain. It was never found, so I bought another, which was about fifteen years old when it sat on the delicate little cushion in the Registry Office. Before George put it on my finger, I remember seeing a piece of soap stuck on the side where I had last washed my hands. It was a simple ceremony and afterwards, we had a brief look around Epsom town and then drove home to cook the lunch and resumed the normal routine. I do recall that we went out for a meal in the evening. The boys were quite amused. We told nobody else. If I am really honest, I did feel trapped and a little sad; I felt as though I had lost my independence.

Every now and again George would have a massive clear out of things which he considered to be rubbish. He would have a bonfire and burn things that I did not think needed to be destroyed. As fast as he came back for more to burn I nipped out to rescue some treasured possessions, both mine and the boys, and stash them away for a while until the heat had died down. It saved a lot of arguing.

On one occasion when the weather was bad, George decided to clear out his old magazines and paper work. Rather than take it all outside to burn he set fire to it on the large old open fire in the sitting room. All went well until he found a cushion which had seen better days. He threw it on to the flames and some of the smoldering feathers wafted up the chimney and settled in an old loft where they used to smoke the bacon years ago. Of course it was not long before they caught fire and smoke billowed out into the bedroom upstairs. We had to dial 999, and being on the borders of Surrey and Sussex, two fire engines arrived along with fifteen firemen. They quickly managed to extinguish the fire and stayed for a while to make sure it was all out. I had a job to find enough cups to give them all a cup of tea. I had managed to rescue most of the bedding before the smoke became too dangerous to stay in the room. For months later anything else that had been in the vicinity absolutely stank of smoke.

In 1980 we celebrated being together for 25 years by going for a holiday to Ireland. We toured round the south and I fell in love with Dingle Bay. We went greyhound racing and spent an amusing day watching gypsies wheeling and dealing at a horse fair. We were impressed with the relaxed way of life the Irish seemed to enjoy, possibly helped by their consumption of delicious Guinness.

In 1984 we went to Cornwall for a few days and stayed in a friend's house right by the harbour at Mevagissey. It was lovely to watch the fishing boats coming and going and to see how aggressive the gulls became whenever there was food around.

In 1985 we had the kitchen refurbished and a few other alterations made to the house.

By then, there were grandchildren and step-grandchildren on the scene. The cupboard under the stairs was full of dressing up clothes. They had fun parading about in them, often playing kings and queens. I remember one day Simon did not fancy being a king, so he knelt down on the floor and covered himself with a large blanket and announced that he was a stone.

Apart from John, who was married and living in the flat and managed the farm, the other three boys had flown the nest. George announced that he no longer wished to play nursemaid to a herd of cows. Changes were afoot once again.

CHAPTER 21

A Chapter of Accidents

In his spare time, John became a genius at bringing life back to redundant motorbikes, and he had converted a couple of old dumped cars into buggies to run round the farm in. It was a relief, once they were all adult that I no longer had to worry where they were or what they were getting up to – or so I thought.

Walter, John's old school friend, was working on the farm with John. He had bought a go-cart in pieces and asked John if he would help re-assemble it and get it running. John happily agreed. One afternoon when they had finished milking the cows, the time had finally arrived to give the machine its test run. They had spent hours repairing the engine and putting it all back together. Both their girlfriends were watching and waiting in anticipation. This was the moment they had all been waiting for.

February the 8th 1981 is a day I will never forget. Walter had taken the go-cart down to the bottom of the hill, where being so low, it had grounded on one of the speed humps. John had run down the hill after Walter and helped to dislodge it. They swapped places. Walter followed as John drove it back up the hill towards the house. I was in the kitchen clearing up, when I heard it roaring up the hill. It streaked past the window at speed, then suddenly, there was silence. I knew something was wrong. I rushed out into the yard to find John sprawled out on the ground, unconscious, lying in a pool of blood which was spouting from his ears, nose and mouth. His head had hit a solid post, made out of a railway sleeper which was concreted into the ground. We immediately called for an ambulance and ascertained that he was still breathing. Fortunately Robert was working nearby and I'd remembered that a doctor had recently moved into a house in Kingsfold. Robert sped off to find him, and very fortunately the doctor was in, and they returned within a few minutes. The doctor had an emergency bag packed, complete with a saline drip which he administered without delay. He then took a blood sample to establish John's blood group. Once the ambulance arrived he travelled with John and directed it to The East Surrey Hospital, as Crawley was low in stock of the correct blood group. The others followed the ambulance by car.

Over the next few hours we tried to make ourselves believe what had happened while we waited for news. We were in a state of shock as we cleaned up the blood. Robert and George examined the crumpled go-cart in the workshop. It had an automatic clutch. They discovered that the throttle had jammed open and the brake mechanism had failed as John came over the brow of the hill into the farmyard travelling at an estimated 60 miles an hour. There was a tractor with a cement mixer attached, parked in the yard, so there had not been enough room to pass through. In a split second decision, the side with the post had been the better of the two evils.

At 2 o'clock the following morning, we had a phone call from the hospital to say that because they had been unable to stop the haemorrhaging, John was being transferred to the Atkinson Morley Hospital in Wimbledon. David drove John's girlfriend and me up to the London hospital. We had a police escort for the latter part of the journey. Mr Pickard, the Consultant, was called out and papers had to be signed to allow him to perform an operation which was to insert two metal clips into the artery that was causing the problem. John's skull was severely fractured in two places.

We were warned that even if John came out of the coma he would probably suffer from brain damage due to the loss of blood. He remained in a coma for seven days and was given the drug Quari, known for being used by natives in blow pipes to kill their enemies. It stopped John's breathing. They continued his respiration mechanically by other means to ensure that the blood he had left was well oxygenated. His girlfriend stayed with him throughout. We were all waiting for news. George was so worried that John would be severely handicapped and I remember him saying rather emotionally that if that was the case, there would always be something he would be able to do on the farm. I was touched by his rare display of feeling.

John had no recollection of events when he finally came round, only of dreaming about a large JCB tractor and the chief of police. He had a terrible headache, double vision, tinnitus and a piece of cartilage sticking out of one ear, but incredibly he had no brain damage.

The right hand side of John's face was paralysed. John remembers that a few male nurses would ask him to smile and then laugh – he later realised that he looked strange when he smiled with a lopsided smile! He had to take medication for the terrible headaches, and to ensure that he did not suffer from epileptic fits. The only other injury was a gash on one leg. Once he was on the road to recovery he was transferred back to The East Surrey Hospital, where he recovered remarkably quickly. When he could walk the length of the ward he was allowed home, which was just a few days before his 21st birthday. He was painfully thin, and looked much taller. He had lost three stones in weight.

John continued to suffer from intermittent severe headaches and a clear fluid had begun to leak from his right ear. Part of his face was still paralysed. When I first contacted the hospital they suggested giving him stronger pain killers. I knew they were just fobbing me off, so I insisted that I speak to Mr Pickard, the surgeon, who had saved John's life. I eventually managed to speak to his helpful secretary at St. George's Hospital. Once Mr Pickard received the message he remembered the lad on whom he had operated at 5 o'clock on that February morning and arranged for John to be admitted immediately into a private room. The next day he was taken by ambulance to The Atkinson Morley Hospital for tests. They stuck needles in his face and around his ears and passed electric currents through to find out which nerves were working and which were not. The following day Mr Pickard and his Registrar operated behind John's right ear. They then corrected the ear ossicles which stopped the clear spinal fluid leaking from his ear. They also removed some crushed bone to free the nerve that was trapped between the two fractures.

Once John had come round from the operation, Mr Pickard showed him the x-ray of the two metal clips he had put behind his nose on the night of the accident when he had arrived in a coma. Once again we thanked Mr Pickard for his dedication and skill, and he commented what a challenge it had been putting the ossicles back together.

John had to do many facial exercises and gradually the paralysis disappeared. His face became normal but he still suffered from tinnitus with a loud ringing in both ears and his hearing was reduced by 20%. He was monitored at St George's Hospital every six weeks as they were very interested to see the results of their facial repair operation, and John was told to ring any time if there was a problem.

Before John was allowed to drive again, he had to attend a final appointment at The Atkinson Morley Hospital. The night before the appointment his girlfriend said she could hear a rushing, pulsating noise in John's ear. When John told the doctor he listened with his stethoscope and was told to return a week later for an investigation under a general anaesthetic. They inserted a catheter in his groin and pushed it up through the arteries into his head, releasing a dye which could be detected by x-ray.

It showed up as a fissure in an artery surrounded by veins. There was concern that the hole would increase in size which could cause paralysis down the left side of his body.

Ten days later John was admitted to The National Hospital, in Queens Square, London, where they intended to put a catheter with a balloon attached up through the artery in his neck and release the balloon over the hole. His girlfriend went with him and remained there throughout the operation. Unfortunately all did not go according to plan. The balloon floated off and blocked the wrong artery paralysing him down one side of his body. We received an urgent telephone call asking for permission to perform the five hour emergency brain operation needed to remove the offending balloon. John, being interested in mechanical details, later discovered that they used a circular type of saw set at 45 degrees to remove a piece of skull to gain access. They were then able to locate and remove the balloon. The piece of skull was then replaced and held together with clips.

The anguish of having to wait and trying to discover how things were going was unbelievable after all he had been through, just as we thought everything was going to be alright. We all visited him in turn, but there was nothing we could do except be patient and give it time.

It was two days before John was conscious enough to know what was really going on. He awoke to find that he was strapped to the bed with tubes coming out from various parts of his anatomy, an excruciating headache, and the pulsating, rushing noise was still present in his right ear. He was furious when a group of doctors explained that they had inserted another balloon beside the fissure and that it might flap across the hole in time. After another brain scan they discharged him. John was not impressed with the treatment he had received at The National Hospital compared to the other three hospitals that had treated him previously. He had felt totally isolated, largely because the staff there were all senior nurses and not at all friendly.

One afternoon after being at home for several weeks, the pulsating, rushing noise began to falter, but the pain increased. We phoned the hospital and again they said to take stronger pain killers. The noise had almost stopped, but he was in agony. We checked on him through the night, then when he woke up in the early hours the following morning, the throbbing in his head had cleared, with much less tinnitus. The balloon had finally flapped over and closed the gap. Over the next few months and years the headaches gradually subsided, and John was able to return to normality and farming again, much to everyone's relief.

Four years later, in 1985, Ricky took off to Australia to work his way round the country and gain experience down under. He found a good job on a massive farm in the outback.

It was seed drilling time and the points on one of the huge machines needed changing. Ricky accompanied the foreman and another employee out to where the work was in progress. In order to accomplish this job, Ricky was required to go under the machine. While he was underneath, one of the other men climbed up onto the tractor which was still running, to acquire some more tools for the job. In doing so, he accidentally knocked the tractor into gear. It slowly ran over Ricky, crushing him into the ground, fracturing his shoulders and crushing his chest with multiple bruising and damaging his vertebra.

Fortunately Ricky was still alive, perhaps because the ground was very dry and he had been pushed down into the sandy soil. It was lucky too that the foreman had a little knowledge of first aid. Being in the back of beyond, they strapped him to a board and bumped him over rough ground for many miles, to the nearest place where they could contact help. He was then given pain relief while waiting to be flown to a hospital in Esperance, where he stayed for several weeks while he recovered. The doctor said that he was very lucky to have survived – being young and fit had been an advantage. It was fortunate too that he was able to contact a family who were related to local people back home in England. He stayed with them until he had fully recuperated.

Ricky's accident was a devastating blow, coming so soon after all we had been through after John's accident. It was a terribly worrying time, especially as Ricky was so far away. The only good thing was that by the time we heard about it, we knew he was over the worst and were able to keep in touch by phone, as of course it was before the Internet was available. I had been on the verge of buying a ticket to Australia, but to my great relief we were assured he was making a good recovery.

He came home via Canada, where he stayed with his half sister Mary, George's daughter, who was married to Keith, a doctor with a medical practice on Vancouver Island.

It was a wonderful day when he arrived home in one piece.

ELIXIR

Once in a while,
when a turbulent day
has dashed me
into a vortex of confusion,
I seek refuge
in the cool night air.
With harsh wounding words
echoing my deflated ego,
I wander through the wood
under the ancient trees,
growing conscious of a coalescence
between earth and man's entity.

Lured by the moon's radiant charm to the hill crest,
there sensing a magnetic influence
beneath the star spangled sky,
all facets of my personality
unite in unison with the universe.
My spirit rises for a euphoric moment,
transcending into timelessness
where past, present and future are as one.

My soul regenerated
I can once again
face society's rigid disciplines
conforming to routine and time.

14ᵗʰ September 1982, written when many changes
were taking place in my life.

CHAPTER 22

The Break Up

Towards the end of the 1980s my relationship with George had really broken down. It resembled a volcano; many times issues would almost become fully blown, then gradually things would calm down again and the air would clear. In 1989 the volcano came to a head and finally exploded into a full blown eruption.

It had been quite obvious that George was seeing someone else, all the signs had been there for everyone to see for a long time, but he assured me it was all in my imagination. He spent even more hours at the pub and was drinking and gambling heavily. The boys were all over 25 years old and happily paired off. There was no one else left at home to share the syndrome of whipping boy, and I alone took a torrent of verbal abuse every time things did not go according to plan.

Many times he told me that I was going senile when I referred to events but he could not remember what had actually happened. An example was when once the bullocks escaped from their field. Several of us had helped him to round them up and put them back. The next day they had managed to break out again. When I suggested to George that they had possibly escaped from the same place as the day before, he told me, "You're going senile, those bullocks never got out yesterday." He was beginning to have blackouts. It was very confusing; he would say something one day and completely reverse it the next. He really was becoming a Jekyll and Hyde. The boys had always referred to it as 'the dipstick effect', according to how much alcohol he had consumed.

Whenever we had friends round he would be rude to me in front of them, saying the most outrageous, degrading things, always trying to put me down – more so than usual when he had an audience. The only way that I could stop it from embarrassing the visitors was to make out that it was a joke and laugh it off with a slick comment.

The last few years with George had become like living in a warzone. I would be so livid with his behaviour that I would inflame the situation by arguing. It was like banging my head against a brick wall. With hindsight, it would have been better simply to have walked away, but once I was fired up, it was not in my nature to give in.

In the Spring of 1989, I went to Switzerland for a holiday with Robert, Trisha and their family. We stayed with my grandmother's relations and met our other Swiss relatives. It was a welcome break and I stayed on for a while after the others had returned home. It gave me time and space to think about my future. I began to realise how I had allowed George's behaviour to take its toll on me.

I began to reminisce over my life with him, about those times when he had been violent. He had given me black eyes and bruises, and on one occasion a broken rib. Once he took a dog's choke chain from a drawer and placed it round my neck. I was not quite sure how far he would go, so for once, I managed to stay calm and quietly talked him round. I was released unharmed, although, I must admit that my heart had suffered from rapid palpitations!

I have to confess that my own behaviour left much to be desired. On many occasions over the years I had fought back, often in devious ways. I remember one occasion early in our relationship when I hid his false teeth. George's usual routine was to go down to the pub for a pint after a hard day's work, while I was left to put the children to bed and did all the jobs that can't be done with little ones around. Usually he returned at about 10 o'clock for his supper. Once in a while, like a horse, he would kick over the traces and not return home until the early hours of the morning. I would start to get angry. On this night, I had been very busy, wishing that I too could have time off to enjoy the company of other human beings, in centrally heated surroundings, with television, instead of being shut away, miles from anywhere, in a freezing, ancient farmhouse. 10 o'clock came, 11 o'clock came, then midnight; by this time, my blood had risen to boiling point. Livid is not a strong enough word. Just before 1 o'clock,

I heard the sound of his van coming up the drive. Shortly afterwards the downstairs door opened and the stench of alcohol wafted up the stairs before George finally emerged, crashing into the bedroom, completely Brahms and Liszt.

He normally left his revolting false teeth overnight in a special cup on the window sill above the kitchen sink, but this time I awoke in the morning to find his false teeth grinning up at me from the bedside table. I thought it might be a little more subtle (and would save having an abrasive dispute) if I chose actions to speak louder than words, so before he awoke I hid his teeth. I enjoyed the scene that followed. He couldn't remember where he had put them. He searched high and low for them. The following day I watched, with a wicked sense of satisfaction, as a very embarrassed George plucked up courage to drive down to the pub to face all his mates, with his front teeth missing, showing just two fangs, resembling Dracula.

I felt that justice had been achieved, without an ugly confrontation. I hid the teeth under the bed and suggested that the children, who were still quite young, play hunt the teeth to see who could find them. Young David came down jubilant and claimed the reward of a shilling and a pat on the head. The truth never came to light.

I remembered the times when he became furious if meals were not ready on time. He was still in the Victorian era, when the little woman was expected to be at the man's beck and call at all times. He would come home from the pub. All the pots would be on the Aga, almost ready to serve but if it was five minutes late, he would ask, "Are we having any dinner today?" My hackles would rise yet again.

Many times, when lunch had been ready and waiting on time, he would be up to three hours late. Once when he was inebriated and eating his lunch with a stupid grin on his face and the peas from his dinner plate were rolling onto the floor, I was so furious and could not hold my tongue. I remarked how childish he looked. He threw a glass of water at me, and when I said, sarcastically, "You see what I mean?", the glass followed.

Another time when he arrived home very late for his supper, he came in drunk and presented me with a bunch of bent stalks and a few broken flower heads, as a peace offering. They were the last remnants he had grabbed from a flower seller's bucket. I felt angry and insulted, and threw them out of the window. These scenes do sound amusing, and if written into a soap opera probably would be, but there was definitely nothing funny about living them in real life.

I re-lived an evening when I came home and was met by David who, still living at home, was about to go out. He advised me to check on his father. David had managed to put him to bed but he was concerned at the state that George was in. I did not rush but I left it for a while, until after I had fed the dogs, then I went up stairs to check on George. I peered over him. He appeared to have stopped breathing. In the next few seconds all sorts of thoughts flashed through my head. I was about to investigate further by testing for a pulse before phoning for help, when George suddenly gave one almighty snort. I retreated with very mixed feelings.

Over the years George became more like Scrooge. When we finally had mains electricity he replaced all the sixty watt light bulbs with forty watt ones, and gave the boys a wallop if he caught them with the electric fire on in a room that was not heated. Then he started to add water to the milk churns on a Sunday, when no tests were carried out – to pay for his booze. I thought he was beginning to go too far, especially as he was very frugal with the house keeping. We had never been short of food because we had always produced our own milk, eggs and vegetables.

I began to wonder where all the money was going and one day when the weekly bill from the bookie dropped through the door, I thought a little investigation would not go amiss. I steamed open the bulging envelope. My suspicions were well founded when I discovered that on one bet alone he had put £2,000 each way and also paid another £400 for the tax. The rest were smaller ones. I carefully resealed the envelope and never uttered a word but resentfully realised that this was money for which we had both worked very hard. Although sometimes he did win, it was time for me to keep my hard earned money from my greyhounds separate and leave him to play with his. Once a month I paid him for all expenses connected with rearing the greyhounds, the milk, electricity and telephone calls and also for petrol until I had bought my own car. We both signed and dated the amount of money I had given him, to prove that it had all been paid for. It kept him from saying I had not paid and trying to get me to pay twice.

I tried to remember the good times when we worked so hard to try and make a happy home for the family, but even then bringing up children in those days was still mostly the mother's job in which he played no part, having done his hard day's work outside on the farm. Over the years he had been very hard on the boys. If any of them had been off colour or ill they were allowed just one day off work. It was always a joke, as they were told to enjoy their one ill health day, while it lasted.

Once back home from my holiday I sought advice. My doctor was very supportive and said that if I left, I would probably go through hell but would no doubt come out the other side. She suggested that I contact Al-Anon, a group that runs in conjunction with Alcoholics Anonymous, although the meetings were held separately. It was formed especially for family members or people living with an alcoholic. My first meeting was a real eye-opener, and gradually I realised how I had actually been feeding George's behaviour, putting myself firmly in the position I now found myself. It was such a relief to talk with people who understood.

A member of the group suggested that I chat with someone from Farm Place, a clinic that I never knew existed. It was in a beautiful country house with tranquil grounds in Ockley, just the next village. I made an appointment to go there and the lady who interviewed me said that I would be accepted. She added that in her view I would benefit from a few weeks in residence there, whatever the cost. I was suspicious and thought that it may be a con but went away and pondered over it. I made a few enquiries and gave it much deliberation: it was a huge decision that I alone had to make. Farm Place was expensive but by then I could afford it and decided to go ahead.

I quietly made arrangements and gave George one day's notice that I was leaving him. For old times sake we spent my last night at Wattlehurst back in bed together. In the morning I left and never went back to live in that ancient house, so full of memories, again. It was a huge wrench leaving behind everything I had worked for over thirty three and a half years.

On the 22nd of November 1989, I walked through the doors of Farm Place. It was the most massive experience of my life. I met very many interesting people; some very wealthy, professional and influential, many were celebrities, others from various parts of the world. The lives of them all had become traumatic in one way or another. Most had become reliant on alcohol or drugs to see them through. Others were obsessive. At that time there was just myself and one other lady who were not using drugs or alcohol. We had in common that we had unknowingly allowed ourselves to be on the receiving end of the damaging behaviour of those we lived with. I fully realised that my own behaviour had hardly been exemplary. We were there to take a hard look at ourselves and try to change the way we reacted by learning to walk away and focus on our own lives and behaviour, rather than wasting it trying to control another.

The rules at Farm Place were strict and we followed "The Twelve Step Programme". Each person had to prepare and read out to the group an honest, detailed account of their whole life. All of the life stories were highly confidential. The feedback from all present could be quite harsh, to say the least, with around twenty-eight people and counsellors giving feedback over several weeks on how they saw us, sometimes contributing suggestions as to the best way forward to make our own choices. It was not easy for those who had been addicted, especially those who had been on drugs. Watching them cope with their withdrawal symptoms was sad. Some said they had the sensation of snakes crawling under their skin.

Life at Farm Place was like being in a big family. Not everybody was amicable; some were downright irritating and difficult to communicate with. There were lectures, films, group meetings and talks every day. The house, grounds and surroundings were beautiful. The food was excellent and being in such a close community there was plenty of company, with so many interesting and diverse people with whom to chat and share experiences. Trust, Risk and Share was one of the mottoes. We were not allowed outside of the grounds, although there were no locks to stop anyone from absconding. There was a fine gym, tennis courts, croquet and a swimming pool.

On Mondays, everyone was given their chores which had to be carried out each day for the rest of the week. For those few who had never done a day's work in their life, it came hard. Breakfast was one of the meals that had to be prepared by a pair on the roster. Usually, one who hadn't a clue how to cook was paired with someone who could. The main meals were prepared by a chef and kitchen staff.

On Saturday evenings we made our own entertainment, which was great fun. On Sundays, families and friends came to visit and were asked to contribute anything that they wished to say, whether good or bad, in front of everybody, about their relative. I was grateful to the family and friends who came to visit me. Many had been shocked at my disappearance. It was then that I found out who my true friends were. One surprising visitor was Fred, a local man who was a friend of the family. He had heard through the grapevine that I was in Farm Place.

After nine weeks George had not made any contact, so was asked to come and see one of the counsellors. He turned up and, typically, was annoyed that he was kept waiting. However, he finally admitted that he did care, but no longer loved me, which was no surprise. You can never change a person; they have to do that themselves, and only then if they really want to.

I'd had time to stand back and see the wood from the trees and finally understand my situation.

Farm Place gave me the tools I needed to fix my problems, to understand the interplay between an addictive personality and consequent obsessive behaviour. I now knew that a co-dependent has the choice whether to feed into that behaviour or not. I discovered how to recognise when things become out of balance. I was shown that it is possible to sort out problems amicably with a change of behaviour by both parties, although very difficult when fuelled by alcohol or drugs. Most animals have a peck order to establish control, and human beings are no exception. We can learn to use tact and to choose not to react. We should communicate honestly, to say how we feel, to become assertive not aggressive.

At Farm Place I had finally found the person I really wanted to be, I had found me.

I believe the Serenity Prayer expresses perfectly the invaluable lessons I had learned, and it is worth taking the time every so often to think about the message it conveys.

Grant me the serenity to accept things I cannot change;
courage to change the things I can
and wisdom to know the difference.

I stayed on at Farm Place while I made arrangements, trying to remain positive about the next chapter in my life. I had become a much wiser person.

For the first week or two after I left, I went to stay with some friends to adjust to the big wide world again. I felt shattered, as though I had been taken apart, pruned and put back together again. Gradually, I emerged as though from a chrysalis, ready to start my new life.

Finding Me

I had tried for years
and shed many tears,
trying to please my alcoholic.
We both worked hard
but life was marred
by his behaviour and his frolic.

I could do no right,
he kept money tight
much spent on gambling and liqueur.
The family grew
and sadly I knew
for them Father cared but a flicker.

We all took some flack;
when he arrived back
we'd be showered with verbal abuse.
As hard we all toiled
my anger fair boiled,
true reasons I denied by excuse.

I ranted and raved,
my sanity saved
by study at evening classes.
I buried my feelings
decorating the ceilings
and striving for O-level passes.

I was really obsessed
as I knew he caressed
others from not far away.
My confidence crashed
as hopes and dreams dashed
I was livid when all he would say;

"It's all in your mind,
don't be such a bind -
everyone drinks and has fun.
Like it or lump it
I'll have my crumpet" –
it's a good job I hadn't a gun!

My drive was all gone
when I found Al-Anon,
a life saver – it cost not a dime.
They were all very kind
as they heard me unwind;
they nodded "live a day at a time".

If you use some tact
learn not to react
all your troubles will soon become less.
It's happened to me
but soon you will see
it takes courage to change a life's mess.

'Farm Place' I then found
and there went to ground
to learn more about looking at me.
I cleaned bogs and bins,
confessed all my sins
very slowly began then to see.

It's all a disease
stop trying to please,
you're powerless over all but yourself.
Your attitude change
which may seem quite strange,
don't feel guilty or left on the shelf.

Just trust, risk and share
Farm Place will be there,
rely on your gut feelings true.
Rock bottom's a hole
where you'll find your soul,
now stop feeling depressed and so blue.

My emotions felt scrambled
as around 'Farm Place' I ambled –
wished the earth would swallow me up.
Go share in the group,
then have some good soup
talk to others like you while you sup.

I'd felt in a cage
for such a long age,
door open – I was frightened to fly.
But now I'm aware
to balance and care,
have courage, be honest not sly.

I accept my emotions
without pills and potions,
a higher power I've found at long last.
No gender has mine,
it helps me cope fine
I'm grateful the grief has all passed.

I pass the tools on,
suggest Al-Anon
to those not too blind to see.
I meet my friends there,
we trust, risk and share.
My own person am I – I've found me.

This poem was written to share with Al-Anon members, to help others in similar circumstances.

CHAPTER 23

Moving On

I had found someone to look after my mare, on the condition that they were able to have a foal from her in payment for her keep, which was one worry solved. I was sad to leave the Shetland Sheepdogs behind, but I knew they would be well looked after as George was fond of them too.

I had to find occupation for my independence, and of course needed to earn some money. I signed up as a Country Cousin, and was sent to look after a lady who had just had a hip operation. She had a farm and had kept horses in her younger days. She was amused that I had been a veterinary nurse, but was quite happy for me to nurse her. We had a lot in common and became great friends. I stayed with her until she was fully recovered. I went back a second time some months later when she had another operation.

I looked after her dogs too. They were real characters. One was a very large, young lurcher, the other a cheeky, elderly, little whippet, who would whip anything off the table if we didn't watch her. There were two dog beds, one by a radiator and the other in another corner of the room. If the lurcher was on the bed by the radiator, the whippet would bark madly, pretending there was someone at the door, and when the other one leapt up to investigate, the little whippet would then dive onto the centrally heated bed. Last thing at night they were each given a bone shaped biscuit to go to bed with. The whippet would eat half of hers and would bury the other half to tease the lurcher, daring it to venture near enough to take it. Her hackles would rise, she would growl and show her teeth but had always eaten the biscuit by the next morning.

David and his wife Theresa were very supportive. They took me to see shows in London and we went on holiday. David had bought some land adjoining ours and had started a transport business. Robert and Trish, his wife, had kindly let me stay with them in the farm bungalow which we had originally built for a cowman. It was at the bottom of the farm drive, where they had started a plant nursery.

I had been recommended to see a London solicitor to sort out the divorce. He advised me to change the locks and move into the second bungalow which had been built for George's mother, after his father had died. She had stayed with us while it was being built and then was happy living in it next door to Robert and Trisha until she passed away in her eighties. George then rented it out, but the moment it became vacant again, I moved in. It was only partly furnished, so once again I lived very frugally with a plastic garden table and chairs at first, until I found just what I was looking for at a car boot sale – a beautifully polished table and four smart chairs. I bought them for a reasonable price from a pleasant couple who even kindly delivered my purchase for me.

The boot sales became my hunting ground for other household things I needed. I then started trading myself, selling rescued plants from Robert's nursery. I originally started selling plants after the 1987 gales when so many had been damaged. I had rescued hundreds and nursed them back to life before I sold them. I then carried on selling small and surplus plants. It became an enjoyable and lucrative hobby.

In between times I continued working as a Country Cousin. Jim and Joyce, the couple who owned Farm Place, had to go to America and they asked me if I would look after Joyce's parents while they were away. The elderly couple lived in a bungalow beside Farm Place. It worked very well for me, being so close to home. I was still able to do the odd Friday Market and car boot sale because there were plenty of people to keep an eye on my charges in the day time, so long as I went back to sleep there at night. I'll never forget Joyce saying that if I could manage to drive a car towing a horse trailer I would certainly be able to manage to drive her parents' brand new Jaguar car. I was very apprehensive. The gardener gave me a short lesson when I drove him in the Jaguar to pick up his newly repaired car from a garage – he then left me to drive the Jaguar back alone. It was the first time that I had ever driven an automatic car. Fortunately I managed to park it in its garage without any hitch, and after that I was engaged as chauffeur and took the couple wherever they needed to go. I dreaded parking it up in multi storey car parks, it was a nightmare, but luckily passengers and car remained unscathed.

I twice went to look after a lovely lady at Oxted, in Surrey. She'd had an operation on her foot. Her twin daughters, who were my age, lived abroad. She treated me as though I was one of her family and it was enjoyable looking after her. I used to take her shopping, and we often went to her friend's house for a delicious afternoon tea of smoked salmon sandwiches and scones with jam and cream. The friend was a jolly, retired army Major who had some very interesting tales to tell. It was fascinating adjusting to different routines and cooking in someone else's kitchen.

The second time I went to help her was when she had been diagnosed with cancer. It was so sad helping her sort out clothes that she knew she would never wear again, and heartbreaking watching her strength slowly ebbing away. She was such a charming, brave lady.

I was beginning to feel that I was coping well with my new independent life, but then one winter evening I had a frightening experience in my car.

The weather had turned colder in the afternoon and frost had been forecast for later. I was driving down through a wooded area when I realised the road was already frozen and tried to slow down. The car skidded on the ice, zig-zagged across the lane, over the verge, down into the wood and crashed into a tree. I was knocked out for a moment or two and when I came round, I felt as though I was in a fairy tale. The car lights were shining down into the wood and it all looked and felt so surreal, I thought I was Red Riding Hood! The engine had cut out and it was another moment or two before I realised what had happened, and that I was in my car. I managed to open the door and turn off the lights, then staggered up the bank to the lane and was heading for the main road when a lady in a car came along. I waved her down and she kindly gave me a lift back to my son David's house.

David took me to hospital. The nurse thought he was my husband which was quite amusing in spite of the circumstances. I had to have an X-ray and the results were rather disturbing because although I had not sustained any life threatening injuries, they discovered that I had what at first I thought the foreign gentleman kept calling 'Badgers Disease'. It eventually dawned on me that he was trying to to tell me that I had Pagets

Disease in my skull. It is a bone disease which can affect older people, and my Mother had it in her pelvis. The bones soften and old growth does not reabsorb. It was something that I did not want to hear, especially just after the accident. However, David took me home and I stayed the night. The next morning my buckled car was rescued and my life resumed as normal, with just a few bruises.

To date, I have never again felt I was in the middle of a fairy tale.

CHAPTER 24

Settling into the Bungalow

The divorce was not actually finalised until 1994, but I had already taken the solicitor's advice and in 1990 I moved into the second bungalow at the bottom of the drive. It was strange watching George going up and down to the old farmhouse with his new partner – the one he'd assured me many times was a figment of my imagination – who he later married.

The only things that came back from my old home were a small antique table, a few plates and dishes and a very prickly cactus plant which I had bought at a village fête when Robert was two years old. My diaries appeared to have been burned. Only half of the Greyhound and Horse Trophies with my name engraved on as breeder were returned to me. One day when I had watched everyone from the farm go out, I drove up to the house and managed to climb through the kitchen window and rescued my other trophies, along with a little pepper pot from the kitchen table which Ricky had given me as a present when he was very young.

Once I knew that the bungalow was definitely to be mine, I gradually began to make it more homely. I decorated it throughout and added a few more knick-knacks from the car boot sales. It soon became cosy and comfortable, especially when sacks of logs began to arrive at my door during the cold winter months. A little note was attached to the first one, saying that it was from The Wood Fairy. At first I was mystified, as nobody had been seen delivering them. Then I suspected that it might have been Fred, who lived just one mile down the road and had visited me in Farm Place. My hunch turned out to be correct, and it was not long before he invited me for Sunday lunch. It was the start of a wonderful relationship, filled with wildlife, wasps and a wicked sense of humour.

Fred was born in 1920. His father had been a corn merchant in the city and his mother's family were hoteliers. He was the youngest of five children. Gladys, his eldest sister by twelve years, had a big hand in bringing him up. She had taught him his manners which were impeccable most of the time, and how to clean his teeth, which gleamed whenever he grinned. He grew up on a farm near Horsham, spending much of his time alone with his dog, watching wildlife. He was a student at Collyers, which in those days was the local Grammar school. On leaving school he trained to be a game keeper, which suited the outdoor and country life that he adored.

In 1939, just before the outbreak of war, Fred qualified for the Life Guards and was one of the last to be trained to fight on horseback. He spent time at Windsor Castle guarding the Royal Family when Queen Mary was still alive and the present Queen was just a young girl. While still a dashing young cavalryman he learned how to ballroom dance and enjoyed the tea dances that were then in fashion.

At the outbreak of World War Two, Fred was involved in the evacuation of Dunkirk and later was with one of the first battalions of troops to cross the channel at the time of the invasion. That was a gruelling experience, but worse was to come when his regiment was sent to help deal with the barbarous atrocities of war. Fred was put in charge of a batch of German prisoners who were given the dreadful task of helping to clean up Belsen concentration camp and the gas chambers. He had witnessed all the terrible horrors on the way, seeing dismembered bodies of people and animals blown apart, some dangling high up in the branches of trees, but watching the corpses being buried at Belsen was heinous. Many of the victims had been so malnourished and ill that it was possible to pick up their carcasses one in each hand ready for mass burial. Later, Fred spent time with the medics in the hospital at Belsen, keeping a watchful eye on the German prisoners who had to help nurse the remaining victims, many of whom were only just alive, terribly damaged, both mentally and physically. While he was in the hospital he learnt chiropody.

Subsequently, Fred was given a break and enjoyed a stint in the catering department. He could prepare a fantastic meal from the hoof to the table, with all the trimmings. Later he was put in charge of batches of German prisoners back in this country. For that job, Fred maintained that he needed eyes in the back of his head to watch what they were up to. In his last months of service he graduated into Administration and Intelligence.

Man's inhumanity to man and the atrocities he had seen left a lasting, gruesome imprint on Fred's memory. He suffered nightmares from the experience for over twenty years. In those days there was no support for troops when they were demobbed at the end of the war.

When Fred left the Army he found it difficult to settle down. He built a bungalow for the girl he hoped to marry, but sadly it never happened, so he sold that bungalow and bought his "little patch of England" as he called it, which consisted of a cottage, surrounded by ten acres of land, with a wood of ancient oak trees, a brook on the boundary and six acres of grazing pasture. He lived alone with his dog.

Fred never married although he had never been short of girlfriends. He had been friendly with the village nurse but she had sadly died a few years earlier. He started up a successful business as a Tree Surgeon, and could climb up a tree like a monkey with all his climbing gear on. He employed sixteen men. Later, his game-keeping expertise came into its own when he was much sought after as an agricultural vermin contractor, which is how most local people, including me, came to know him. He often did work for nothing; money and material things meant little to Fred. He was a strict disciplinarian, often outspoken, a man of his word, a good listener and had a dignified charm. He was always the same, and he usually had a joke or a story to tell. He had planted a quarter of an acre of daffodil bulbs in one of his paddocks, and every spring when the daffodils were in bloom, he visited many of his customers delivering large bunches of daffodils and I had been one of those lucky ones.

We became soul-mates. Living just a mile apart was ideal, we were comfortable popping in to see one another when passing by. Fred was happy and contented living on his own with his hunt terrier Tiger for company, and rearing chickens and ducks. He had a set routine. I too enjoyed my independence, being able to come and go as I pleased, but we were always there for each other, caring and sharing our daily happenings. We never had a cross word. Fred said what he meant and meant what he said. He was a true gentleman.

I continued with my markets and on Sundays, after my car boot sales, Fred would have a roast dinner ready for me upon my return. Later I would help him clean through his cottage. Then we would do any outside jobs that needed attention. Like a couple of children, we often played Pooh Sticks, as in the famous Christopher Robin Stories, where we would each throw a stick into the brook and watch to see whose stick rounded the bends first. When we were coppicing in the wood and burning the rubbish, we made chimneys out of the large hog weed stalks for the smoke to rise up through. Then finally we always took Tiger for his walk by the brook, where he would investigate all the rabbit holes. In the evening we watched TV. Just after the 10 pm news, Fred would suddenly leap up shouting, "ACTION!" It was supper time and he would bring me my supper, all neatly laid out on a plate. Tiger and I were quite good friends but after 9pm he didn't like me sitting in his chair which was next to Fred's. I had to sit very still if Tiger chose to sit on my lap to share the chair. He would growl if I made a false move. He was a very fiery little fellow. I became friendly with Fred's sister, Gladys, who was in her eighties, and a very strong, positive, character. I used to give her house a clean through too, once a week.

My mother who was also in her late eighties was beginning to suffer from dementia and my father who was then in his nineties, although still very able, needed a little extra help. I became very adept at cleaning as I used to clean the house for them also, and made cauldrons full of soup to divide up into meals for the freezer. Once a week I took them shopping and my sister, who lived much closer, used to do the laundry and would always be on hand whenever they needed help.

One day when I took my father to the supermarket, we were in a queue, waiting to pay for our shopping, when my dad, who still had an eye for the ladies, seeing a very slim lady in front of us blurted out in a very loud voice "Good God, look, look at that, if she farted she'd blow away." It was funny but oh, so embarrassing!

One night when my dad was not very well I stayed the night and my poor mother decided at two o'clock in the morning that she was going to a wedding and started pulling everything out of drawers looking for something to wear. I managed to coax her back into bed and tucked her up tightly. At five o'clock she was calling out that she couldn't move. I hastily released her, but at least we had all had some sleep. Much of the time she was quiet and easy to manage, but we always had to keep a watchful eye on her as she had been known to try to boil the electric kettle over the flame of the gas stove. On one occasion we attended a dear friend's funeral, and we all went back to a beautiful old farmhouse for the wake. It was a glorious sunny day and we had met many friends whom we had not seen for years. When the family were seeing us to our car to say goodbye, my mother said that she didn't know when she had enjoyed herself so much. It was a poignant moment.

Soon after she had a fall and had to go into hospital. One of us visited her most days. We were not happy with the treatment she received and having just finished a course on assertive behaviour, I complained to the head of the hospital management and a meeting was called. The head man was aggressive but the other four sat quietly and listened to what I had to say. I was trying hard to remember all I had learned at my classes. I did mention calmly that in my view, the animals I had worked with at the local vets and also at the veterinary research centre received better treatment. At the end of the meeting the boss stormed out but one of the other ladies came up to me and said how pleased she was that I had said what I did. After that episode my mother received excellent treatment. Thankfully, the respite care home where she later stayed, treated her very well. In 1994 she sadly died in hospital, at the age of ninety- one.

Care in the Community

The finance cupboard is so bare,
there's little money left to spare
for old and worn there's often no place,
to rest, reflect and find solace.

Surviving war, trauma and loss,
now left feeling just like dross.
Haunted by memories, grasped by cold,
hungry, lonely, curse they've grown old.

Someone suggests "Community Care",
but finding help is one nightmare.
Social service is a real maze,
leaving the elderly in a haze.

It's fine for those who can still shout,
but sad for those who've lost their clout.
If at long last help is found,
kind nurses, all creeds and colours abound.

They wash and dress and help you up,
they're meals on wheels when time to sup.
If very lucky you may enter,
the benefits of a day care centre.

Alas! at worst you have a fall,
an ambulance then comes to call.
Four hours in agony you wait,
until the X-ray yields your fate.

A fracture to the lower leg,
unable to cope, a bed you beg.
Staff pass the buck and looking harassed
state, "There's no bed, we are embarrassed".

At last a vacant bed is found,
The patient's now reduced to a mound.
Confusion, bitterness, frustration
they well sedate with medication.

Specs are lost beneath the locker,
can't find the bell or any knocker.
Teeth grinning from behind dead flowers,
left on the loo for what seems like hours.

Can't see the food upon the tray,
and so begin to waste away.
No hand is given to wash your face,
rushed nurses like robots running a race.

A distant relative appears,
proclaims you've really lived your years.
They wonder if you've made a will,
its "Now, my dear, just take your pill"…

Although the funds are so depleted,
It's degrading how our old are treated.
Why do so many have an immunity?
Where is the Care in the Community?

Written in 1993 and published in the Surrey Mirror, at a time when my poor Mother was admitted to hospital after a fall and I was feeling very frustrated and disgusted at the poor care she received.

A few weeks after her funeral, I called into a friend's house on my way home from selling plants at the Friday Market in Horsham Town Hall. I had some pansies to deliver for her and stayed for a cup of tea, a doughnut and a chat before popping in to see Fred, who lived opposite. I returned home in the early evening, unloaded the empty crates and watered the unsold plants. When I unlocked and opened the front door, a strange plastic bag was lying near the doormat, which I thought was odd.

I went into the kitchen and to my horror found that the window had been forced open. With a pounding heart, I gingerly ventured into my bedroom where I found all my belongings scattered over the floor. The drawers had been turned out and my box of jewellery and sentimental treasures ransacked. I tried with difficulty not to panic, took a big deep breath and phoned the police. They calmly took brief details and assured me that someone would be along shortly and not to touch anything.

A bigger shock ensued when I went into my study. My locked, leather briefcase had been hacked open with a knife, and I discovered later that all my bank details, debit card, passport, birth certificate and other important documents were all missing.

The police assumed that the burglar had been disturbed while in my sittingroom, because the glass door of the cabinet where my silver racing trophies were kept was open and a couple of them were out on the floor, but nothing in that room had been taken.

A friend working at the nursery, who came to be with me while waiting for the police to turn up, remarked that the burglar would more than likely return for the trophies, something which, I have to confess, was not what I wanted to hear. The police arrived and carefully noted all details; another came to take finger prints. It appeared that no one had seen or heard anything suspicious. They advised me to inform my bank and to cancel everything immediately, which I did. That night Bruno, my son's dog, spent the night with me. He slept in his basket in my bedroom. It was a long time before I fell asleep; every little noise startled me. Bruno just snored!

The next day when I phoned the bank to sort out my details, the person on the other end of the phone was very curt because, having had all my papers stolen, I could not answer all her security questions, and she refused to go any further. The Police put me in touch with Victim Support. I was so grateful to them. They sorted it all out with my bank manager from whom I received an apology. The thief had managed to take two lots of money from my card before it was cancelled.

The culprit was never apprehended and none of my precious belongings were recovered. Fortunately, I was insured but no amount of financial compensation could replace the sentimental worth they represented to me, or appease the shock of realising that there could be another person walking around with my birth certificate and all my other personal particulars – the thought of that was just a little bit scary!

CHAPTER 25

My New Life

I found I was enjoying my Sunday car boot sales and my blossoming friendship with Fred. I established a busy routine and confidently began to move forward in my new life.

Friday was my Market Day at the Horsham town hall. The markets became a lucrative and enjoyable sideline. Sometimes I chatted to customers or other folk who just liked to browse. Any spare time in between, I used to sort out and clean up the plants by taking any yellow leaves or dead heads off and reviving any that looked a little down. My garden flourished too. I rescued and planted all the very bent and buckled plants that were too damaged to sell. Within a few weeks, the ones which managed to survive rewarded me with a magnificent show of colour.

I had a pleasant holiday with my sister when we drove up to Fifeshire in Scotland. Our cousin Mariette's eldest daughter Linda was getting married. The wedding was spectacular, the reception was held in an ancient castle. While we were in St Andrews we revisited all our old haunts which we remembered from childhood holidays and our evacuation there during the war.

With the proceeds of the markets, I could spend time with my family when they went skiing. I first ventured on to the ski slopes at the age of 58 and continued for several enjoyable seasons in both Switzerland and Italy. Once when the weather changed and the snow suddenly became very icy, I really thought that the "blood wagon" would have to bring me down, the going had become so treacherous. I was just an amateur and had travelled much higher on the chairlift than my capabilities for the descent allowed. However, Ricky saved the day. I had to lock my skis into the back of his and hang on to him for grim death. He brought me safely down at breakneck speed. I was terrified, my legs felt like jelly. I managed to fall off the button lift twice but was fortunately rescued by a very handsome young man on both occasions.

I accompanied Robert and Trisha and their family to Holland several times. The Dutch Plant Auctions covered a huge area and were very interesting. Many of the plants arrived in the UK a little later on the same morning. I also returned to Switzerland with David, Theresa and their family, where we stayed with our Swiss relations and visited many places of interest on the way, including a fascinating salt mine that went for miles underground.

A visit to Cornwall with Theresa and the children was another enjoyable short break.

Holidays were not for Fred; he had seen enough of the world and was content and grateful for his little farm, but whenever I came home from my trips abroad I would always find a beautiful bouquet with a note attached to welcome me home. It was so heart warming and I appreciated his gestures very much.

In 1994 after our mother died, my sister and I were concerned as to how long our father would be able to cope alone. He was 93 and had been managing amazingly well. Although upset at her funeral, he was soon busy tending his garden again and was still able to drive his Hillman Husky car, which he kept in pristine condition. We need not have been too worried because it was not long before we discovered that he was having a regular visitor. We then realised that Betty, his long term girlfriend, was still on the scene and had been for over 65 years. In the 1920s, when he first came down from Scotland to join the Reigate Police Force, he had been friendly with her older brothers and used to help Betty to cross the main road when she was a young girl on her way to school.

It all came to light when Dad had become a Master at Arms on the Union Castle Line after he had retired from the police. Betty had been going to meet him off the boat as Dad had always told Mother that he docked a day later. Somehow she found out what was really happening and was absolutely devastated. Mother was very ill when I was born and I rather gather from what my father confided in me shortly before he died that sex had not been on Mother's agenda after I came along.

All the time my sister and I were growing up father had been strict, but very caring. No matter what questions I asked, he would always give me an intelligent answer and encouraged us to be interested in all things. I think he had wished that I had been a boy and inherited and shared his engineering skills. I used to try to help him by handing him spanners and other tools when he was busy under the car. There would be the odd expletive when things were not going according to plan, but when there was a serious problem he would let rip with a loud outpouring of dreadful swearing which echoed out from under the bonnet, at which point I would drop the tools and take refuge back indoors until the air had cooled down. He did have quite a quick temper which we always blamed on his Italian grandfather's flammable bloodline.

When my sister was in her teens, she used to upset father by correcting his Scottish accent. She would ask him "Do you mean your Worship?" when father was explaining about a court case and had pronounced the word 'Worship' as 'Warship'.

There was one memorable occasion when my sister and I were well in our teens and we were squabbling over who was to cook the smoked haddock for tea. My mother came home just in time to see my father, having had enough of my sister's sarcasm, take hold of her by the neck, leading her to retaliate by screaming " Murder, Murder," hoping to cause a scene for neighbours to hear. Her head almost went through the glass of the back door. I stood by secretly thinking she deserved what she was getting but my mother was calling for father to stop. He was persuaded to release my sister, and peace was finally restored.

When I was ill after Richard was born, it was father who actually looked after him early in the mornings. He was always very good with the other grandchildren when they went to stay with them on odd occasions, and it was my mother who took them to the swimming baths each time they went to stay with her and taught them all to swim.

It was when my sister and I began to rebel a little in our late teens that he felt he was losing control and no doubt he probably worried that we would find out what was really going on in his life. It had been a case of not practising what he preached, because he had told my sister to find other accommodation when at the age of nineteen she disobeyed his orders to be home by midnight. The parents of her friend had brought her home from a party, just ten minutes late. The next morning father told her to go.

It was different with me because, back in the 1950s being pregnant out of marriage was such a disgrace, it wasn't unusual for a father to demand a daughter choose to leave the family home if determined to keep her baby. He also told my mother that on no account was I to enter the house while he was away at sea. She dutifully adhered to his wishes, but her mother and sisters were always kind and welcoming.

My sister and I always knew that father had an eye for the ladies. It all came to light when one evening I quietly came through the back gate just in time to see someone climbing over our garden fence into the neighbour's garden. My sister and mother were indoors at the time. It was very odd. Suspicions were confirmed when much later father made a little door in the garage loft; it overlooked the drive. He said it was for ventilation but one day I thought I would investigate what he had stored in the loft. I managed to climb up on to the bench then lift myself up with the help of an ingenious folding bar he had made. To my surprise, right at the back of the loft, I found a comfortable mattress with a bottle of wine lying nearby. Father didn't drink wine! Also, neatly laid out beside the little door, were some postcards and a few other interesting bits and pieces. It looked as though a stranger had been in residence.

Things all fell into place when we realised that many times he said that he had work to do on the car, or was just going out to fill it with petrol, but now we knew there was much more to it than met the eye. However, once Betty appeared, as though from the woodwork, we understood that she had helped to keep Father's spirits up, especially while coping with mother in the latter stages of dementia.

In September 1994 my cousin Mariette, whose husband had recently died, wanted to visit her brother and a sister in Canada. My step daughter, Mary, lived on Vancouver Island so we decided to pay them all a visit. I flew up to Scotland and the next morning we boarded a plane at Glasgow Airport for Canada. It was my first trip across the Atlantic Ocean. We landed in Toronto and met Randolph, her youngest brother, for a few hours, while we waited for a plane to Vancouver. It took another five and a half hours in a packed plane, with considerable turbulence, before we finally reached our destination, and hailed a taxi to take us to the hotel.

On our first morning in Vancouver we went on a coach tour. First we visited an Indian reserve, continued on to Grouse Mountain and then on to a river where we watched salmon leaping up out of the water, swimming back to their place of birth ready to spawn.

Our hotel appeared to be on the edge of the red light district and very late on our second night there, some windows were smashed in a break-in to one of the sex shops almost opposite. The police arrived and arrests were made. By the morning the glass had been replaced and all was quiet once more.

The next morning Mariette went to visit an old school friend, and I boarded a boat to Vancouver Island to visit my step daughter Mary and her husband Keith. On the trip across the water I was immensely lucky to see a school of killer whales leaping up out of the water. It was an unforgettable spectacle which only lasted a few minutes; they appeared to be playing. Mary and Keith had lived on the island for over twenty years and had been out many times hoping to see them, but had never been so lucky as I was on my single crossing. I spent a few wonderful days on the island and then Tara, their daughter, accompanied me back to the mainland and I met Mariette again.

The next morning we caught a train to Edmonton to visit Mariette's eldest sister, Connie. It was a long trip but we spent much of it in the observation coaches while we travelled through The Rockies. They were so beautifully wild and rugged. We stopped for a break in a memorable little town that appeared to be in the middle of nowhere called Jackson. I wished we could have stayed longer, it was so intriguing. The rocks were of a colour and shape so different to any I had ever seen.

Many hours later we arrived in Edmonton and met Connie and her family. We stayed in a five star hotel with a revolving restaurant overlooking the city.

Connie and her family took us on tours around museums, botanical gardens, the main shopping centre and many other places of interest. After several days there, it was time to head back to Toronto by train. It was a long trip through miles and miles of corn growing country. We were met there by Mariette's eldest brother, George, and his family.

Toronto was a little like London, massive and very cosmopolitan. I have never been happy surrounded by buildings. While we were there we visited The Niagara and Horseshoe Falls which were magnificent. We also visited the folk who still prefer to live in the past, called The Mennonites; they have an interesting way of life and still use horses instead of cars and dress in an old fashioned way. They were charming people. We visited a hospital for children and toured round Toronto. My cousins gave us a wonderful holiday. It all passed so quickly and all too soon it was time to say our goodbyes and catch a plane back to Glasgow.

Once in the UK I spent one more night in Scotland and then flew back to Gatwick. Robert met me late in the evening and I arrived home and found another beautiful bouquet on the table from Fred, who was my first visitor the next morning.

CHAPTER 26

The Roller Coaster Years

It was good to be home again, and to be with Fred. I soon settled back into my old routine, but dark clouds were brewing on the horizon. One day Fred called in after he had been to the doctors. He had just received the results from tests that had been taken a week earlier. I will never forget how shattered he looked when he whispered "I've got prostate cancer". It was a horrible shock. I felt so helpless, there was little I could do except be there for him.

In the Spring of 1995, things were becoming very bleak when out of the blue I had a pleasant surprise. The phone started to ring with various folk from the horse world congratulating me on having bred Flashing Steel, the winner of The Irish Grand National. Charles Haughey, the then Irish Toiseach, had bought Flashing Steel for a considerable amount of money after the horse had won several top class races, including running fourth in The Cheltenham Gold Cup. I had no idea that he had been running so well. It was a wonderful surprise at such an anxious time. I had bred and reared Sabre, as I had nicknamed him, but had sold him as a youngster ten years earlier. Fred was interested in the horses, especially as he had been in the Horse Guards. It was good that he could enjoy it with me and it was a welcome lift just at that time.

It was quite amusing how people like to know you when something like that hits the headlines. When I went to a meeting for thoroughbred breeders later that year, the Irish kept stroking me, hoping some of my breeder's luck would rub off on them. It had been the same when Wattlehurst Rogue, the greyhound that I had bred and reared, won the Wimbledon Puppy Derby back in the 1960s. People that I never knew came to celebrate as though they were friends and had known me for years. I hadn't a clue who they were, but it was fun being famous for five minutes.

For a while Fred was able to carry on as usual, but gradually the cancer began to take its toll. He was given medication and a nurse called in quite frequently. She told him that he was living with, not dying from, cancer. However, the next time he saw the specialist, Fred was told that he didn't have long to live and should sort out his affairs. Our strolls beside the brook together with Tiger became very treasured moments indeed. One day in December I found Fred plodding slowly back to his bungalow with a spade in his hand. He had just buried Tiger and was very upset. Fred's visible grief at the loss of his feisty little companion was the saddest sight to behold.

The Christmas of 1995 was tragic, and Fred knew it would be his last. He was so brave. Early in February Fred went into St Catherine's Hospice as he was so ill and unable to eat. I visited him every day. On the afternoon of 18th February 1996 I was shopping for my Dad in a supermarket in Reigate when I received a call from the Hospice to tell me that Fred was fading. I phoned his sister who lived in Horsham to tell her the news and to say that I would pick her up and take her to see Fred. He was still conscious when we arrived and Gladys, herself by then almost ninety, was able to spend a little time with him before saying her last goodbye. I took her home and then went back to be with Fred, who was in considerable pain despite it being controlled. He whispered to me and I held his hand until he lapsed into unconsciousness and slowly passed away. The staff were so kind and caring. I lit a candle for him and then made the very sad and lonely drive home.

All my family were fond of Fred and had been to visit him before going off on a skiing holiday. The funeral arrangements were postponed until they were all able to attend. He was cremated, then afterwards everyone came back for the wake at the Nursery where one of the empty greenhouses had been beautifully decorated with plants and flowers and set out with tables and chairs. The food was wholesome and skillfully home-cooked by some of the Nursery staff. Fred would have loved it. Later, Robert bought a special upright oak tree in memory of Fred which we planted down beside his bungalow, on his little patch of England, which he wanted me to have and look after. I planted two weeping willow trees close by, one for Fred and one for me. A week or two after the funeral, on a glorious sunny afternoon when the daffodils were in full bloom, I took the urn with Fred's ashes and walked slowly round scattering them in all the places he loved. Then I buried the urn with the remaining ashes beneath Fred's special, ancient oak tree which he had said was his favourite spot, from where he could view the whole of his patch. I have the most wonderful memories of Fred, and always give him a wink when I dust his photographs.

With a most ironic twist of fate, early the same year George was taken ill. He went into hospital for an operation to fit a new heart valve, but never recovered from the operation. On 3rd February, just two weeks before Fred's death, he too died. George's daughter Sheila came down from Scotland to stay with me to attend his funeral. I accompanied her to the Church, but we sat discreetly at the back. The Vicar mentioned that George had been "quite a character"! I secretly felt that a large tranche of his "character" had been left out.

The weeks and months following Fred's death dragged by slowly. David's dog Bruno, a chocolate coloured field spaniel, frequently paid me a visit, arriving via a hole in the hedge. He was good company and I used to take him for a walk in the woods, trying to come to terms with having to live without dear Fred. I continued with my markets along with helping to look after my Dad and cleaning for Fred's sister. It was my Dad who gave me some good advice when I mentioned to him that I would like to see a little more of the world. He told me to do it while I was still young enough to enjoy it and not to wait too long. I was then in my sixties. I heeded his wise words and my cousin Mariette and I went on some wonderful adventures.

In 1998, having given myself time to think about the next chapter of my life, I decided to let Fred's bungalow and to build stables on the land where the remains of an old barn stood. Fred had already mentioned that it was an ideal place for stables for my horses. David had kindly built me a temporary winter shelter for them in his yard because the paddocks at Fred's were clay, becoming very muddy in the winter. Very muddy conditions can cause mud fever, especially for horses with any white haired legs (which mine had), possibly leading to serious complications if not monitored carefully. My friend and vet Colin had suggested that an American type barn would be the best option, allowing everything to be under one roof keeping man and beast dry in bad weather. With John's help I carefully planned the best way to develop Durfold Hill Farm, Fred's legacy to me, into a small stud. John eventually built the American barn for me. With its three paddocks leading into the yard, it worked very well and enabled me to continue my passion of breeding thoroughbred horses for racing. I was fortunate to be able to call on my friend Ena's daughter to help when I had difficult horses to deal with. Stella has an extraordinary ability to communicate with and handle temperamental horses – she was my own private "horse whisperer"! Ena and I spent happy times watching her perform her magic.

CHAPTER 27

Up Up and Away

Mariette and I had so enjoyed our trip to Canada that we decided to venture into unknown territory further afield, so we booked a Baltic cruise. I flew up to Scotland and spent an evening with her family, then the next morning we flew from Glasgow to Holland to pick up The Costa Allegra, a large Italian cruise liner, which was to be our home for the next ten exciting days. We were given an impressive welcome aboard and later shown to our cosy cabin. On the first evening we were introduced to our 'Maître d' who was in charge of the excellent waiter service. We met our table companions while sampling our first sumptuous meal on board. After the meal, we made a quick tour of the vessel to find our bearings and then booked all the conducted tours that we wished to make, making sure that we would be accompanied by an English speaking guide. There was plenty of entertainment; a Variety Show, a Casino, Music and Dancing were all in full swing before we turned in to our cabin for the night.

The next morning we sailed through the narrow Kiel Canal that divides Germany from Denmark. Our first stop was Gdansk in Poland where we spent an interesting day wandering through the city, watching young children skilfully playing musical instruments in the main street for money and, rather alarmingly, others trying to sell porn magazines. The port was busy with containers being loaded on and off huge ships that were docked in the harbour. The next day we visited Gotland which is a small island that currently belongs to Sweden. Two facts about Gotland that have stuck in my mind are that it has thirty churches, some of which we visited, and curiously that the suicide rate was very high.

The next day we went to Tallinn in Estonia, a beautiful, interesting old city. We visited one of the ancient cathedrals where, tucked away in a dimly lit corner, a funeral service was taking place beside an open coffin. In the afternoon we watched a concert performed by attractive young dancing girls, dressed in their national costume. The following morning we arrived in St. Petersburg where we spent two days. There was plenty to see in the churches, museums, and art galleries. St Catherine's Palace at Pushkin was truly magnificent, beautifully decorated, much of it gilt-edged with real gold. Guards sat in every room, keeping a watchful eye on the visitors. Catherine the Great's life appeared to have been a very interesting one. She had many lovers, leading to numerous pregnancies. There had been much speculation about how her husband Peter the Great, who was several years her senior, had died. However it was thought that she brought much wealth to Russia by carefully selecting her lovers. One was said to have given the Russian Navy a boost, while others had much to give in other ways.

In spite of all the grandeur in the places of interest, many of the people, roads and pavements looked to have seen better days. Water draining from the high buildings splashed on to uneven pavements through broken pipes. In some streets, the tram lines were just hanging in place by loose gravel. It was 1995 and it looked as though Russia was still picking itself up from very hard times.

The markets were interesting and it was fun to browse. Russian dolls, which graduate down in sizes to fit inside one another, along with trinkets and knick-knacks in abundance were displayed on the various stalls. In the evening I went to see my first ballet, which was The Nutcracker. It was beautifully performed. At the interval I was surprised to learn that the lemonade I chose to drink was more expensive than the vodka! Once back on the boat we usually had a choice of meals from the countries we were visiting and delicious caviar was on the menu for supper that night.

I loved to watch the little tugs as they carefully towed us out of each harbour and into the open sea. At dawn the next morning we arrived in Helsinki, passing by many delightful, small islands, each with one or two holiday homes known as Dachas. Finland appeared to be sparklingly clean and tidy, in vast contrast to the bustling streets of St Petersburg. We visited a church which had been created within a cave. We toured round, absorbing the interesting way of life of the Finnish people. Our guide mentioned that the menfolk were very conservative with their emotions, quoting an old adage that if a man said he loved you on your wedding day, it would probably be the first and last time! Perhaps it is something to do with the cold climate.

The next day it was Stockholm. We visited the Parliament Buildings and investigated the smart surrounding areas. Everything appeared to be well organised, very similar to Copenhagen in Denmark, which was our last stop in Scandinavia. Here we visited the famous gardens and I watched some crazy, daring youngsters bungee jumping from a massive, towering crane which jutted out over a quiet corner of the harbour.

That night we sailed back across the choppy North Sea to spend a day shopping in Amsterdam, and finally we cruised back to Dover. Mariette and I both agreed that the truly spectacular holiday had been money well spent.

In 1996, later in the year after Fred had passed away, I accompanied Mariette to her comfortable family holiday cabin overlooking Loch Ruthven, not far from Inverness and the Scottish Highlands. We spent an enjoyable time catching up and swapping notes on our family, and Scottish history. We drove to Culloden where a very bloody battle had taken place back in April 1746, between Bonny Prince Charlie and King George II. One of our ancestors, who belonged to the feuding Davidson Clan, was reputed to have swum across the River Tay to avoid capture. That side of our family had been strict Covenanters who held secret meetings – some had been politically involved.

The name Mason was thought to have once been Manson and originated from the captain of a Norwegian ship that had been wrecked in a gale off the coast of Largo, close to St. Andrews. The Masons were blacksmiths for over 500 years and in our grandfather's day they still had two working smithies at St Andrews. Most of the intricate wrought ironwork around the university buildings, along with the railings, had been created by them. When our grandfather married a Swiss girl, it caused much dissent within the family and our father's grandmother did not want much to do with her grandchildren. If they visited her, she would tell them in her Scottish accent to, "Run away hame, there's gangerals aboot."!

Her youngest son was her favourite and the rest of the family, nick-named him Sugar Ecky. However, he rather shamed himself in later years.

While studying theology at St. Andrews University, he was responsible for a fellow student becoming pregnant and left for England in disgrace around the mid 1800s. There had been an extremely unpleasant fracas when our grandfather paid a rare visit to his mother's home to retrieve his violins. The violins were valuable and were his pride and joy. The Masons were a very musical family and played at weddings and other special occasions.

Our fathers had been no angels. When they were little boys, mine blew air into the gas pipes at the church where the family sang in the choir. It caused a stir when all the lights went out, resulting in him being instantly dismissed as a choir boy. When in his early teens, Mariette's dad punched his boss and knocked him out for calling him a bastard. The male members of the family were heavily into boxing before they went their separate ways.

We reminisced over the war years when we were together for a while. Mariette's mother, my aunt Mary, often used to feed us all. The children were fed on the first shift, and the adults ate later. Her mischievous brother, Albert, set fire to his slipper when he tried to light up and smoke a stick of cinnamon. We remembered with affection our dear grandmother with her strong Swiss accent. She made cauldrons full of hot peppery soup which she served to us in little pudding bowls. We used to sit round on stools, and on the wall above us hung a large Swiss clock, with a cuckoo that popped out every quarter of an hour announcing the time.

People seemed to be much more hospitable in Scotland than people in the south. One was always welcome and their houses were always open to visitors, but down in the south a calling card was often expected, stating the date and time of arrival.

There were many other stories. We had heard about the many poor souls who had been declared witches. They were not witches of course, but they were burned at the stake nonetheless. This went on right up until the end of the 1700s. It was condoned by the authorities who made a fine profit once they had confiscated the land, goods and chattels which had belonged to the unfortunate slaughtered victims. One of our distant relations had suffered from this heinous crime. Another tale was of a young mother of ill repute, who dosed her bairns up with a drop of brandy before she went for nights out on the razzle-dazzle. But the bairns were believed to have been very well fed!

Mariette had many tales to tell. Our fathers had a tough time growing up because they were considered foreigners, but they were big and strong and could hold their own. They all did well in later life. William, my father, came south to join the Reigate Borough Police. Mariette's father George married Mary, a lovely girl from the Highlands and they emigrated to Canada where he became a fur trader up in Hudson Bay and also in St. James's Bay, where Mariette and her siblings were born. They grew up alongside the Eskimos. Fitz, the youngest brother, went to Alaska and later joined The Canadian Mounted Police for a few years, then went to Toronto University to study mineralogy before going gold mining in South America and later diamond mining in what was then known as The Gold Coast – now Ghana- in Africa. In his old age he wrote a fascinating book about his travels, called 'Beyond The Horizon'. George later returned to St. Andrews with Mary his wife, Mariette, her sister Connie and their three brothers. They wanted their family to have a good Scottish education. When the children first arrived back in Britain, they were not familiar with our farm animals and thought that the cows, sheep and pigs that they saw on their journey back to Scotland were very strange creatures.

Mariette later went back to Canada where she met her husband, who also came from Fifeshire in Scotland. They then spent some time in Africa before they too came back to educate their family of three boys and two girls in St Andrews. Mariette was an accomplished pianist. I remember her playing with great gusto the well known tunes of their times. The Twelfth Street Rag is the first one that springs to my mind.

It was interesting to see how various family traits often surfaced again through the generations, and still do. Engineering and music seems to have dominated much of the male line. The Masons developed a door lock and also a hot water system.

For our last holiday together in 1997 we chose a trip to China. We flew to Beijing which was very regimented and strictly Communist, but very interesting with such a vastly different culture. While in Beijing we visited Tienanmen Square and the Secret City, also a nursery school where we played with the cute little children who entertained us with their singing and dancing. We then moved on to another district and visited a jade factory. While there, some of us crept round a corner to investigate a covered market where we saw huge bottles of maggots and a massive jar full of unfortunate frogs piled high on top of one another, and a couple of poor dying animals that looked a little like badgers. All these unfortunate creatures were waiting to become someone's dinner. We had seen enough, so quickly retraced our steps back to the jade factory and later went on to a place where they made beautiful ornamental copper pots. Many of the people working in these places had moved in from country districts for the work. They lived in crowded conditions although buildings were going up at an amazing rate.

The air in some towns was very polluted, because much of the power and heating was still produced from coal. The Silk Lane was interesting. It was like a market in a crowded lane which sold all silken items at a reduced price. We also visited a zoo and saw the pandas, which all looked very healthy.

Mariette, who unfortunately had to visit a loo at most stops, alerted me to the procedure of coping in these situations, so I went to investigate. First, one joined a long queue outside. Once inside the door, by then with legs crossed, one was greeted by a strong stench. An elderly lady sitting on a stool issued me with one small square of loo paper which, once it had been used, had to be put in a basket and not down the loo. How vastly different from the luxurious Friendship Hotels we were staying in!

A few days later, we travelled by train further up north and visited The Great Wall and climbed quite a long way along it. The panoramic view was impressive and I was surprised when we looked down to see camels in some places. We were not far from the Mongolian border.

At dawn on the first morning at our new venue, I was awoken by what I thought was the sound of geese cackling. On closer inspection I discovered that a large outdoor market was taking place and still growing. Intrigued, I quickly dressed and went out to investigate – I seemed to be the only European there. I found it so fascinating. Most of the produce arrived by men peddling three wheeled bikes with loaded trolleys, many with the wife perched on top of the load. There was an amazing display there. All the meat, bones and other bits and pieces were laid out in large bowls and difficult to identify. I could only hazard a guess as to what type of carcass they had originated from. There was a wide variety of fresh vegetables, some of which I could recognise. It was a memorable morning – the people were country folk and so friendly. There were a few caged birds. The only time we saw any wild birds was in what had been

Monastery Gardens, which were opened for people to relax in. Some people were doing Ti-Chi, others were exercising. Trying to cross the main road was challenging, as traffic seemed to go both ways at once on the same side of the road. Policemen were everywhere, standing up on pill boxes, trying to keep order, without much success. We enjoyed the entertainment in the evenings which was varied – folklore, an acrobatic display and a Chinese opera.

We then flew to Xian, The City of Eternal Peace that had once been the capital city of China, where at Li Shan Mountain we spent a memorable time visiting The Terracotta Army. It was an amazing spectacle; every single one of the 6,000 figures was different and all created over 200 Years BC. We went on to see a neolithic village at Ban Po, where the dead had been buried in an upright position.

Our last day was spent back in Beijing shopping. The people who were on the same trip with us were a great crowd and it was sad when we had to bid them all farewell. Mariette and I felt that we could have done with another holiday when we arrived home, very happy but exhausted!

CHAPTER 28

Krassimir

The Plant Nursery that Robert and Trish had started at the end of the farm drive was flourishing, and in Spring it became a hive of activity and extra staff were employed for the busy planting season.

I first met Krassimir in the Spring of 1991, when he was on holiday staying with a friend who was one of the nursery's seasonal staff members. I thought he was a very pleasant young man, about the same age as my own sons.

One morning in the Spring of 1997, Krassy arrived unannounced carrying just one suitcase, hoping to find work on the nursery during the hectic busy season. At first it was difficult to find him accommodation, so he stayed temporarily next door to me. One day he was feeling peckish and found a large freshly baked sponge cake cooling off on the table. It looked so inviting that he sampled a small slice. It was so delicious, he cut another piece, which only left a small slither, which eventually followed the rest, leaving an empty plate. For this demeanour, he was asked to find other accommodation. A young couple working on the nursery took him in until somewhere else could be found. He was about to pack his bag and return home when a member of the nursery staff pleaded with me to give him accommodation. So after a little persuasion, I took him in for the summer. He had my spare room. I did not realise at the time that another chapter in my life was about to unfold.

In the autumn of 1997 I had booked to go to China. Krassy went back home for the winter. At Christmas we exchanged Christmas cards. I knew that he was keen to return and mentioned that I may be able to find him extra work. In 1998 he arrived in the UK, became self-employed and stayed with me for the next ten years.

At first his English was very limited. It was fun trying to teach him. I had no idea how difficult our language is to explain, and could not answer why we did or said things as we do, especially to someone whose own language I could not understand. Gradually things began to come together and with some English books for children and a picture dictionary we began to make headway. He worked long hours and having to concentrate on learning our language for half an hour at the end of a hard day's work was challenging for him. It paid off in the end. We had many laughs over some words. I would be talking about juice and he thought that I was talking about Jews. He said he could cook 'hemannicks' which I thought was some special dish from his country; it turned out to be ham and eggs. He thought 'let us', was 'lettuce'. Then often when he phoned I never knew if he was coming or going, as he had a problem with the meanings of come and came or going, gone and went and the little words that go in between. Once we could communicate, things went very well. Problems still arose trying to explain why we have lots of words spelt the same, but mean something very different, such as sow and sow, minute and minute, tear and tear, Polish and polish. When you think about how it is for someone trying to learn English, it is quite crazy!

He came car booting with me and at first he thought that boxes full of odd bits and pieces were rubbish, but it was not long before he realised that it was fun rummaging through them to find little treasures that someone else had cast off. He learned to haggle over their price, then sell them from my stall for a profit at another venue.

In his country it was not done for a man to take orders from a woman and he found it strange to find that it was acceptable in the UK, or that women here often drove their husbands around in the car and even drove horse-boxes and buses. British manners amused him. He enquired, "If I say please and thank you in the morning, do I have to keep saying it all day?"!

We became good friends; I looked after him as a mentor and he looked after me. It was a perfect arrangement. After the Sunday morning car boot sales we would come home and unload the unsold plants and other bits and pieces before lunch, and afterwards I usually had a short power nap to recharge my batteries. Sometimes on sunny days we would go to the sea, or if the weather was too wet for a car boot, and during the winter months, we often went to London. For the first time in my life I went to art galleries; the Science Museum, the Natural History Museum and the War Museum and many other places of interest including China Town. At first Krassy was a little dubious about going deep down into the undergrounds. He did enquire if we had earthquakes in England.

One Sunday afternoon, after a busy car boot sale, we came home and after lunch I gave Krassy a map for him to choose somewhere he would like to go while I had my forty-winks. After my siesta I asked him if he had decided. He said he had never been to an English island and pointed to the Isle of Wight. It was 4pm and a little late to start a journey of that distance, however I thought there might just be time, so we set off. When we reached the ferry most folk were returning home from a day on the island. We had not booked but luckily there was plenty of room on the boat. It had been a gorgeous day and the crossing was very smooth. Once on the island we decided to do a round tour. We stopped for an unofficial swim on an isolated beach, then continued on round. The sun was going down like a ball of fire as we looked out for a memorable few minutes to watch it disappear behind the row of huge chalk rocks, known as The Needles. We continued on round and were just in time to catch the last ferry home. My horses were late coming in for supper that night.

Krassy was keen to see more of the UK, so I decided that it would be a good idea that if he was happy to drive, I would supply the car and the petrol. I insured him as the other driver and things never looked back. On June 11th 2000 we took off for a six day trip, with the help of John looking after my horses. The first stop was to visit a horse I had bred and still had an interest in, which was in Shropshire. He had grown and was looking very well. We carried on into Wales and stayed in The Mount Snowdon National Park. The next morning we visited a slate mine and the museum where we saw hand tools that had been used before modern machinery. We carried on to the Lake District and went for a boat trip on Lake Windermere as well as having a look round the very quaint little town. We toured back out to the coast, past a huge power station and watched massive wind turbines performing in a gale force wind.

After a hearty breakfast we drove on to watch a young couple being married in The Old Forge, at Gretna Green. Later we managed to negotiate our way through a congested Glasgow, and I was grateful that I had been taught to read a map by our retired SAS master while at Sheep Hatch School. Whenever I was not sure which road to take from a roundabout, I just told Krassy to, "Go round again." He kept amazingly cool, calm and collected. He was a very experienced driver, having driven large lorries during his army days before satellite navigation became available. Once out of the built up area we were soon heading up into the Highlands of Scotland. Shortly after, small hills began to disappear and were replaced by magnificent mountains, which loomed up in the distance. We drove on through Glencoe with its eerie atmosphere, surrounded by mystical mountains towering out of the mist all around us. We drove on to Portree in Skye where we stayed. I had traditional Haggis, Neeps and Tatties for my supper. In the morning we toured round The Isle of Skye which was beautiful. We visited the museum and then went on to Ullipool where we watched a ferry boat sailing gracefully off to the Isle of Lewis. The Gulf Stream comes over the Atlantic Ocean and brings warm air from America to parts of the west coast of Scotland. It seemed strange to find palm trees growing in some of the sheltered places.

We drove for miles across the rugged, unrestrained Highlands – not a house or soul to be seen for miles – just a strange noticeable silence. We finally arrived at Betty Hill, right up on the north coast where we spent the night. Although it was late, it was still light being so far north.

The next morning we visited Dounreay Power Station, one of the first ever built in the UK. It had closed down by then, but had a museum which explained how it had worked.

We drove on to John O'Groats and took a few photos at the furthest point from Lands End, then continued down through to Inverness visiting a whisky distillery en route. The production of a high quality whisky owes much to the location of the distillery with its access to local spring water containing valuable and unique minerals. We learned about the age old production process; how it starts with the locally grown barley, its journey to the huge vats, and we listened with interest to the explanation of how much time it needs to mature, which is so important to the process which has made Scottish Whisky world famous. Of course we had a taste of a well matured drop at the end of the tour, which was quite mind-blowing.

We spent time at Lochness. Sadly the monster did not surface for us, however the legend was widely advertised everywhere and excellent for the tourist trade. Blair Athole Castle is a wonderful museum of Scottish life through the ages complete with a bagpiper to welcome visitors. The grounds too were beautiful with an abundance of trees and flowers.

We headed on down to the ancient walled city of St Andrews where I showed Krassy my old school and of course the famous Cathedral ruins, golf course, castle, university and many of the other buildings, steeped in history. We spent time with Mariette and my other cousins and took our 95 year old Uncle Fitz out for supper. He kept us amused with all his stories of the places and events that had happened to him in his life. Krassy sat captivated. We took rather a long time over our meal, and to my horror I found I had a parking ticket when we finally returned to my car. I sent a letter to the parking authorities, explaining how the brown envelope on my windscreen had so dampened my wonderful memories of St Andrews, and they kindly waved the fine. It was amusing and my cheeky letter paid off!

We passed through Edinburgh and the Angel of the North on the way home and were happy and amazed with what we had accomplished in those six days. It was always rewarding being with Krassy because he so enjoyed seeing all that we in the UK often took for granted.

The Scottish trip had worked so well. Krassy had enjoyed being a chauffeur and travelling companion, so I thought we should take an opportunity to visit Ireland to see some of the horses I had bred and sold, which had been transported back to the Emerald Isle , the land of their forefathers for racing. Miltonfield, was one of them. He had won two Irish Cesarewitches and many other top class races. We were able to visit him. He had just won a big hurdle race that week. It was a great thrill to see one of the foals I had bred fully matured and looking so fit and well. His half-brother Flashing Steel was in retirement and, we were assured, living in the lap of luxury in a field beside the great mansion house of his owner in a remote part of Ireland.

While in Ireland my car, which had a Northern Irish number plate, had its mirror vandalised the night we had to park it in the road. There had been a pop concert that evening and it was difficult to find accommodation or parking anywhere in that area. The hotel manager greeted me in the morning with the news – in his strong Irish accent, he told me what had happened and that I was to go up past the Cathedral to the police station to sort it out, which I did. They were very efficient. The outcome was that a few weeks later, I received a cheque for the damage. They had found the culprit and made him pay.

We continued on heading west visiting a peat-bog museum. Krassy had never seen peat before. Miltown Bay, Kilarney, Tralee and all round The Ring of Kerry was breathtaking. The folk we met oozed Irish charm. When we asked for directions and were told that our destination was just a couple of miles down the road, we could rest assured that it would more than likely be ten or more. I took Krassy to my most treasured spot in Ireland which is Derrymans Bay, a magical little cove with a cemetery on a tiny island that becomes surrounded by the sea when the tide comes in. There are ruins of a church which once stood there, still battered by the winds from the Atlantic Ocean. The Irish names on the grave stones are still visible, many were from several generations of the same family.

Standing there with the wind blowing through my hair and the sound and smell of the sea, it was easy to allow my mind to wander back in time to imagine how it must have been. Krassy too was fascinated by the ambience. We spent the night in the village. After a tasty supper of assorted freshly caught fish, we enjoyed listening to the Guinness primed Irish folk singing their country songs, which I love.

We called in at Bantry Bay to watch a fishing boat unloading its catch, then headed on round to Cork and on to Waterford, where we viewed some of their famous glassware, before arriving at Rosslare to take the ferry back to Fishguard in Wales.

We came back through the Welsh Brecon Beacons and home again after another very memorable trip.

CHAPTER 29

High Days and Holidays

In the first week of September every year the world famous Dorset Steam Fair is held. It takes place in over 400 acres of open fields at Tarant Hinton, in the heart of the Dorset countryside.

As a child I remember being intrigued by the power of the huge steam rollers when they came as part of the road repair process. I had always fancied going to the Dorset Fair and Krassy was keen to go, so in September 2000 we paid our first visit and were captivated by the whole show, so much so that we have visited it each year ever since. The atmosphere is unbelievable.

On that first visit, we were fortunate to find a short-cut down a narrow country lane that came out just before one of the huge fields used as a car park. We use that route each year, and it saves us having to wait in a long queue at the main entrance. Once parked and having acquired our tickets we head for one of the all day breakfast marquees. The smell of locally produced food cooking a full English breakfast is appetising and it always tastes divine after the two hour journey.

Once breakfast is over, I say good bye to Krassy, having arranged to meet him at 6pm – that's assuming we do not bump into each other before. The day is then our own to wander as we please.

We have visited the site for so many years I've established a routine based on how much energy I estimate I have to spend, so I start with the steam engines of all shapes and sizes. I enjoy watching all the proud owners, often the whole family including the children, dressed in dungarees, covered in grease, helping to polish the brass parts. The family dogs often wear a red kerchief round their necks just to look the part too.

There are usually around thirty or so show engines, many quietly chugging away with smoke gently billowing from their tall chimneys. All have very grand, strong names like Hercules, and King George. Magnificent old organs are strategically positioned around the show-ground. Many are Dutch and play the well loved tunes from over the last hundred or so years. The music emanates from behind the scenes, where a long thick card with holes punched in slowly unfolds. It is like the recipe that actually controls the melodies. Then every now and again one of the figures on show in front of the organ taps a bell or bangs a drum. They are so clever and fascinating to watch, particularly the original ones, which are powered by steam. Next come literally hundreds of working engines, which work on and off over the four days the show is on, while others are just on display. It is amazing watching the power these old engines have. Some are ploughing a large field, others are pulling heavy loads up a steep hill. There are a few threshing corn, and some breaking rocks or powering huge circular saws cutting up whole tree trunks. Many of the owners wear old traditional workman's clothes, with the black bowler hat and a red cotton scarf.

After a rest on a bale of straw to listen to an organ and eat an ice cream, I feel fully revived and usually wend my way through the collection of old tractors and farm machinery to "Granfer's Marquee" where there are old agricultural tools and vermin traps on display, also some ladies making corn dollies and others busy lace making. There is a collection of vintage cars, another of motorbikes and army vehicles. There are usually two arenas where various things are displayed throughout the day.

Trained hawks cleverly swoop on their prey and sheepdogs show how they round up sheep – sometimes ducks are used instead. There is always an amusing sheep shearing show. The dray horses parade displaying all their shiny brass finery, and working cart horses are ploughing and harrowing in one of the big fields. Blacksmiths show how the horses are shod. I love to wander down memory lane where various collectors have their exhibitions on show, including a cider press in full progress. There is also a large funfair.

In the centre of the whole show is a massive market of old jumble along with many new items for sale. You never know what you might find. There is usually a fortune teller or two. The craft and beer marquee has plenty of entertainment going on, and the food venue is huge with hundreds of delicious samples to try before you buy. It is a wonderful, well organised day out, and it's enjoyable to meet up with Krassy afterwards. On the way home we go for a meal, swap notes on what bargains we have bought and chat about the day's events.

We spent an interesting weekend in Jersey. It was at the time of a Foot – and -Mouth outbreak and full precautions were in place, shoes and boots were sprayed with disinfectant. Meat and cheese were not allowed in or out. We toured round the island and visited the German Bunker Museum and the underground hospital, also the ruined Groznez Castle and The Devils Hole, a deep crater eroded by nature over thousands of years.

The small Jersey, high butterfat cows, with their black butterfly noses were in evidence. It was engrossing to see how they had evolved on their home ground.

On an August bank holiday in 2001 we toured Cornwall visiting various friends who had retired to the West Country. On the way down we stopped off at Dartmoor Prison, located on the bleak moor which has a sinister atmosphere. The museum was interesting, showing various ingenious ploys and stories that had been used by prisoners trying to escape over many years. The sea beside the rugged coast around Lands End was rough but there were plenty of holiday makers in all the popular places on the way there, where the harbours and bays were more sheltered.

We visited a Tin Mine and best of all The Eden Project, where plants from all over the world were growing under a massive covered dome, specially constructed to house the magnificent collection. We came back home through Tintagel and visited the ruined castle with its Legend of King Arthur and stopped off in neighbouring .Devon at Clovelly where donkeys used to plod up and down the steep slope carrying loads to the picturesque little bay by the sea. In Devon we visited David, the elderly vet, and his wife Biddy, who I used to work for. They had retired many years earlier. It was a pleasant reunion, but sadly the last, as they both passed away shortly afterwards.

We saw the New Year of 2002 in by visiting my Scottish relations once again. Sadly Mariette was in hospital, she had suffered a stroke but was slowly recovering.

Krassy enjoyed the New Year celebrations, so much so that after a wee dram too many, he never stopped telling me how much he liked Scottish people.

Later that year we did a quick tour of The Isle of Man. On the boat going out, there was no facility to buy a newspaper to while away the time. The gentleman in the aisle beside me had finished reading his paper, it was on the floor by his feet so I asked if I could buy it from him. He wouldn't hear of me paying for it and handed it to me, Krassy and I were very grateful as it kept us occupied for the rest of the journey. When we were queuing to leave the boat, the gentleman who had given me the paper turned to me and said that I looked familiar. " Horsham perhaps?" I asked, and he said, " No, Warnham," which is our neighbouring village. It turned out that he was our village policeman. I did not recognise him out of uniform. I had only ever spoken to him once before. His wife was from The Isle of Man and they were just going out there on holiday – quite a coincidence.

It was interesting to visit the Parliament Buildings, (the Isle of Man is still independent from the UK). Their flag, the three legged symbol, has a strange history. It was first thought to have been chosen by three kings, back in the 13th century but many believe it goes back much further into the Greek and Mycenae civilization. Some deem it to have originated from a swastika which in the far east represents a symbol of the revolving sun and the fire of life, bringing purity and good fortune, long before Hitler commandeered it as an emblem for his German regime. It is an intriguing story. We visited the TT Circuit and the museum. Motor bikes were very much in evidence, many trying out the circuit.

Whenever I went shopping with Krassy, he spent much of his time in car parks looking at all the expensive cars. It was not long before he had enough money to buy a second hand van of his own. I will always remember the letters on the number plate, they were VHK, which I mused at the time might be easily recalled by remembering it as 'Very Happy Krassimir'. Once he was mobile he was able to put his tools in the back. There was plenty of work around for a handyman and he could turn his hand to almost anything. He was also able to car boot independently which before the e-bay days could be quite lucrative if you played your cards right, and he had the benefit of several years of training.

Krassy's brother came over to stay for a few days. He lived in Bulgaria and it was suggested that I might like to go there for a holiday. Krassy could not have more than a few days off at a time, so after much thought I decided that it would be good for me to go on a little adventure on my own. Krassy and John looked after my horses.

In April 2002, I flew to Sofia. Krassy had arranged that his friend George, a pilot, would pick me up at the airport. I was to wear a flower in my lapel and keep an eye out for the best looking guy there, who would be carrying a bunch of flowers. I must admit that I was a little apprehensive. However, all went according to plan. Yes, George was young and good looking. As we drove through Sofia I really thought we were going to take off, he drove so fast. We arrived safely back at his flat, and later that evening, he and his girlfriend Svetzi, took me half way up a mountain – which was still covered in snow- to a very special Bulgarian restaurant. It was beautifully decorated inside, in traditional style. On the tables were little flags to represent the countries where the guests were from. Ours had a Union Jack especially for me. I felt very honoured. The meal was sumptuous and afterwards they called foreign visitors up on a stage to try some traditional Bulgarian dance steps, then after a little practice session the music became faster and faster. It was great fun.

In the morning Svetzi cooked pancakes for breakfast. Fortunately George and Svetzi spoke excellent English, so communication was easy. I went with Svetzi to the pharmacy shop she owned in Sofia, and was surprised to find antibiotics that had been made by a well known UK firm from Worthing in Sussex. After an interesting morning in the chemist shop, Krassy's brother Demetra arrived to take me to Velika Turnova, the old capital city, a few miles from the village where his family lived. The drive there was absorbing; being in a strange country everything was so different. Sofia was much the same as any other big city but once out of the built up area, the old cobbled streets was like stepping back in time and reminded me of my childhood days. When I arrived I was given a royal welcome and a feast by the family. Krassy's young niece, who was twelve years old, gave a poignant little speech in English, welcoming me to Bulgaria.

It was arranged that I was to stay with George's father Stanyo, a retired Army Colonel. He lived in a flat in Velika Turnova close to Emelia, an English teacher who was to be my interpreter while I was there. I had met her a year before when she and her husband, who worked for The United Nations, had stayed with us for a few days' holiday. Stanyo, my host spoke no English and I spoke just twenty-one words of Bulgarian. He was a jovial, rotund gentleman who made me very welcome. In spite of the language difficulty, we enjoyed each other's company and we managed to communicate well.

In the morning we had yoghurt for breakfast; Stanyo ate a giant sized carton of rich buffalo yoghurt along with leftovers from the night before. I pondered that it might add another inch or so to his girth. Shortly after breakfast we met Emelia in Turnova. Her English was excellent. Stanyo drove us to Dranova Monastery. We looked around and saw the monks chanting then he took us to his other home in the mountains near Gaboron. It was in a beautiful location, with patches of snow visible in some places. We had lunch with some of his relations before we drove on to visit some Roman remains, another monastery and finally we arrived at an amazing village where the water which cascaded down from the mountain was used to power many different crafts as it streamed down through the village. The last use was a massive tub in which to wash large articles like carpets, where the water flowed rapidly through. It was most ingenious. Emelia went home and two ladies came in to cook supper. When they left, I was alone with Stanyo and just my twenty-one words of Bulgarian.

The next day Emelia took me all round Velika Turnova. It was a fascinating historical place. We visited the archaeological museum and climbed up to the castle. Some of the streets in the old part were cobbled and the buildings were quaint, a great attraction to visitors. The ancient church had wall paintings dating back centuries. Bulgaria had once been a creative country with a rich, diverse past. Most of their treasured history has been rescued by the churches and monasteries.

The Thracian era of around 500 BC, was followed by the Romans. In 681 a state was established and the Cyrillic alphabet developed for Slavonic communication, followed by the famous Byzantine Empire renowned for much of its art. Then in 1396 came The Ottoman Empire, when the Turks invaded and remained in power for five centuries until in 1878, after terrible bloodshed, the Russians helped free Bulgaria from Turkish rule. The country was later taken by Germany and then by Russia, who left when the Communist Regime collapsed in 1989. It has been struggling to rise again and appears to be in a more positive situation, having been accepted into The European Union. It is a beautiful country and has much to offer, given the chance.

One evening we visited the castle which was illuminated and the most amazing sight.

Unfortunately it poured with rain so the visit was cut short. I had never seen rain like it. I sheltered under an umbrella, but my shoes were drenched. I dried them out overnight but in the morning I discovered that on one shoe the sole was beginning to part company with its uppers. That morning Stanyo took me to a market because he knew I was keen to see one. At the entrance to the market I showed him my shoe. He put one finger in the air, then beckoned for me to remove the shoe. Stanyo's car was like an Aladdin's cave. He carried tools for every eventuality, including some glue to repair my shoe. While we were sitting in the car waiting for the glue to dry, a gypsy put a hand, which clenched two choppers, through the open window, hoping for a sale. It took me by surprise to say the least, but worse was to come when another wild looking individual thrust a huge sword through the open window beside Stanyo. I was on the verge of making an escape through the door beside me and to run with one bare foot. However with a tirade of Bulgarian words from Stanyo, the man beat a hasty retreat. The market was quite unique, with many tools and strange looking household gadgets for sale.

Later that day Stanyo took me through the Shipka mountain pass to see a famous church, which had been built in gratitude to the many Russians who had sacrificed their lives helping to overthrow the Turks. The main roads were in good repair but the smaller ones were full of potholes, so traffic drove on both sides of the road to avoid them. We had a horrendous near miss with an articulated lorry on one of the bends.

In a small village called Prisova we were heartily welcomed by more relations for another wonderful feast. Stanyo had planned my trips with military precision; the liaison between all the parties ran very smoothly and Krassy had thoughtfully advised them on all my interests.

The next morning for breakfast, buffalo yoghurt was again on the menu along with mushroom soup, salad, milk and honey. Stanyo ate his with great relish. I enjoyed a yoghurt. We then drove north and visited Pleven Museum, which had an English speaking guide and held a detailed history of the Turkish occupation and vividly depicted many terrible gruesome battles that took place over the 500 year rule of the Ottoman Empire. We continued onwards and visited the ruins of an old monastery which had been hewn out of the rocks, then drove on past many vineyards. Bulgaria of course is well known for its wine production, and we stopped for lunch in Russe, which is particularly famous for red wine. The restaurant was at the top of a tall satellite tower overlooking the Danube River, which separates Bulgaria from Romania. It was hazy but we could just see across the river and over the border.

Stanyo had a girlfriend called Petra, and we were invited to her small farm home for another great feast. I was an honoured guest, once again. Some neighbouring farmers were invited to join us, and I found it difficult to work out who belonged to whom. After the celebrations, I stayed the night. Petra's son, a lovely lad in his late teens who spoke very good English, showed me round. It was great to see how they lived.

When I inquired where I might clean my teeth I was shown the trough outside the back door. The shower was a large drum and the water was heated by a fire beneath. The loo was in an open ended shack right at the end of the garden. Inside there were two metal supports for balance and a large bucket below. I was awoken at crack of dawn by the crowing of cockerels and various other farmyard sounds. Once it was light enough to see, I wended my way gingerly up the garden path to the shack at the top, which I fortunately found unoccupied. However as I came down, I met Grandma on her way up. We gave one another a knowing friendly smile and a nod.

It was a large rambling old house, and in a sort of utility room by the back door were some live young hens in a pen, clearly awaiting their fate. The food was very fresh and everywhere in the house was spotlessly clean.

It was sad when Stanyo and I bade them all farewell, and thanked them for their hospitality. On the way out of the village I spotted two old timers sitting on a seat in the sun. Standing between them, appearing to be enjoying the conversation, was a goat. I so wish I had taken a photograph. There was no rush and tear or stressed human beings; life seemed so tranquil.

The next morning I said a huge thank you and goodbye to Stanyo when Demitre arrived with Emilia to take me to Shoeman, the largest stud in Bulgaria. It was part of a project which had been set up under the communist regime to help improve many aspects of agriculture, for crops and livestock. I was interested in the true Bulgarian bred horses. They were black, well built, medium size, around 15 hands, very placid and versatile. I was intrigued to see that there was one Irish thoroughbred there.

There were also buffalo at the centre. Many of the Bulgarian buffalo were becoming inbred, so had been crossed with some from the Far East to improve the gene pool.

We drove on to the Black Sea coastal resorts and visited Varna, Nesabar old town, Premoria and on to Dunes which was the closest we went to the Turkish border.

We came back inland and Demitre drove us way off the beaten track to a monastery beside a beautiful waterfall. On the way he stopped by a small lay-by where there was a pipe with spring water running out. Demitre lit a match and to my surprise the water caught fire as there was gas in it.

We drove through The Balkans and visited a famous historical town house, then on to Plovdiv and its cobbled streets. It was the first time that I had seen tobacco growing.

There were hops and vines in abundance and roses grown to make perfume. We drove through the Rodopees mountains where I saw storks nesting. We spent the night in Velimgrad and in the morning visited Bansko, a well known ski resort. After lunch in Blagoevgrad we walked round the town and saw The American University. We went on to visit the famous Rila monastry and passed through the Rila Mountains. When I saw goats and cattle on the road, I asked why there was no electric fencing to keep the cattle in. Emilia told me that they have trouble with Gypsies stealing them. In the villages, someone takes the cattle, sheep and goats out to graze in the morning and stays with them, bringing them home at the end of the day. The animals are used to the routine and are happy to go back to their own sheds when they go home.

Demitre and Emelia delivered me safely back to George and Svetzi. I took them for a Farewell Chinese meal that evening, and the next morning I was delivered to the airport for my flight home.

My visit to Bulgaria was definitely one of the outstanding highlights of my life.

CHAPTER 30

Refurbishing the Bungalow

In 2004 I decided that it was time to give my tired pre-cast bungalow a face-lift. I planned to give it a brick surround, but before I could proceed I had to seek advice and was told to make sure that the footings were at least a metre deep. Krassy dug down and found that it was the correct depth.

So I went ahead and had the brick surround built around the bungalow, it was re-roofed, double glazed and the little outhouse was converted into a self contained annex. The whole bungalow then had double insulation. When it was completed the builder assured me – with a grin – that I would be able to heat it all with a candle! It became amazingly warm and snug. The kitchen had a makeover too with new flooring and units and a second hand Aga. A little later I had a conservatory added which led out onto a patio which Krassy skilfully created, with a beautiful circular stone feature in the centre.

When the builders had finished their work, I turned my attentions to re-designing the garden. Krassy erected a new fence and a second hand shed. We rescued a greenhouse that someone wanted removed from their premises, and Krassy dismantled it and rebuilt it in a sunny corner where I could grow tomatoes. Shortly afterwards we found two more advertised as free to anyone who would dismantle them. Krassy turned them into a potting and cucumber house. The small vegetable garden remained near the greenhouse. Krassy laid a path round the area beside my washing line. We built a rockery on one side of the conservatory, edged by a gravel path with stepping stones. It was most convenient that Robert's nursery was next door enabling me to plant up the rest of the garden with my favourite flowers, many of which were unsold and rescued from the car boot sales.

Once the bungalow had been refurbished, Krassy's daughter, Isabella, occasionally came to stay in her school holidays; she was a pretty teenager with gorgeous locks of dark wavy hair and beautiful hazel coloured eyes. She loved to cook and quite enjoyed homemade kedgeree and her first taste of British baked beans.

When Isabella came over for her Easter holidays in 2005, Krassy took her for a tour of the UK. It was good that they could spend time together. Krassy had been able to pay for her to be educated at an American school near her home. She was a bright young lady and passed the entrance exam with flying colours. She spoke excellent English and later came over to Aberystwyth University where she attained a degree in Biology and Human Genetics which enabled her to fulfil her ambition to work in Cancer Research. She now lives in Wales with a family of her own.

Once the annex was completed, it was soon occupied by Shemick, a Polish builder. Like Krassy, he too was learning to speak English and it was amusing when he repeated the English words that he was finding difficult to pronounce. If we could not comprehend what he was trying to say, he would repeat them louder and louder, hoping that it would help us understand.

His wife Iza and their little 4 year old daughter Sandra came to visit us several times. Iza was so grateful that she could come and stay that on each occasion she cleaned all my windows and paintwork. The bungalow really sparkled; she was not really a cleaner as she had an important vocation back in Poland.

Shemick kindly plastered two ceilings for me free of charge during the week before he finally returned to his home in Poland, to show his gratitude to me. He appreciated that I had been a motherly figure to him and had given him so much help in the three years he was here. We are still in contact, and he has since built himself a fine new house in Poland and Sandra now has a little sister.

CHAPTER 31

The Travels Continue

In 2002, following my trip to Bulgaria, Krassy and I went to the Scilly Isles for the August bank holiday. We flew over from Cornwall, the first flight for both of us on a helicopter. I could not believe how noisy it was. We stayed on St. Mary's, but managed to visit the other islands. Tresco was beautiful, especially famous for its plants, many of which thrive in the milder climate. On the way home we spent our customary enjoyable day at the Dorset Steam Fair.

Between Christmas and the New Year, Krassy and I drove over the Yorkshire moors to visit some friends, then on to the east coast of Scotland to Aberdeen and the fishing port of Peterhead. We watched the fishermen preparing to go out. The weather was bleak and as we came back through the glens it was snowing hard. We passed through Aviemore, the Scottish ski resort – so picturesque in the sparkling snow. We arrived at St. Andrews in time to celebrate the Near Year of 2003 with a gathering of the clan with my Scottish relations. There were seventeen of us all together. It was a very special occasion as Mariette, who sadly had been left handicapped after suffering her stroke, was able to join us and seemed to enjoy every minute.

On the way home through Edinburgh we called in to visit my step-daughter Sheila and her husband Eric. We enjoyed a Chinese meal together and to finish the evening, Sheila and Eric opened a bottle of twenty-two year old whisky at their home.

My 70th birthday in 2003 fell on Easter Sunday. Krassy and I went to celebrate it in Guernsey. We flew over and hired a car on arrival. We were blessed with a warm and sunny weekend. First thing in the morning we walked down a narrow footpath to Saints Bay – a beautiful and magical little place, hidden away and full of charm – with a deserted sandy beach and a cave with waves gently lapping at the entrance. We went to a special Easter Sunday service at St. Peter's Cathedral which was exquisitely decorated throughout with flowers for the occasion.

Later we toured around the island, visiting the German Underground Hospital and the submarine base and museum, not forgetting to look at some Guernsey cows, which are a pretty golden colour and larger than their neighbouring Jerseys, and don't have the Jersey's butterfly black muzzle.

It was a welcome and relaxing break, and a perfect way to spend my birthday.

In the summer of 2005, Krassy and I decided we would like to visit Orkney and The Shetland Isles. On the way we stopped off for a meal with some of Krassy's relations who lived in The Midlands. Once on the road again, we soon became aware that the car did not sound quite right. By the time we reached Blackpool we knew for sure that there was something radically wrong. We found a Vauxhall garage and left the car with them for repair and hired a brand new one, which had just nine miles on the clock.

We enjoyed looking around the highlights of Blackpool, and then we continued north to re-visit The Isle of Skye, with which we had both become enamoured. We drove over the amazing pass through the mountains to Apple Cross. It was a memorable drive up through the steep, and at times eerie, track that zig-zagged right to the top. Once we had finally reached the summit, it felt as though we were on another planet, surrounded by a sea of strange rocks, with a spectacular view of Western Scotland.

We drove on across the north of Scotland to John O'Groats and caught the ferry over to Orkney. Visiting the famous Standing Stones, we saw evidence that man had certainly been in residence inhabiting it many thousands of years ago. An overnight ferry transported us to the bleak and barren Shetland Islands, noticeably with very few trees. With the help of the Heritage Centres, we delved into the history of several of the little islands.

We learned that the Shetland Isles had belonged to Norway until the fifteenth century when they became part of Scotland. There were still hints of Norwegian culture in evidence in some of the buildings. We came across some Shetland Ponies who were busy grazing on any blades of grass they could find between the heather. A couple of inquisitive ponies thrust their wind-blown, hairy heads through the car windows, looking for tit-bits. We saw sheep on the Island which were very small compared to the ones at home, and we watched the fishermen unloading their catches late at night.

On the way back home we called in to St. Andrews to buy some flowers for Mariette who we knew had not been well. It was sad when we said good-bye, I realised that it could well be the last time I would see her. Mariette died a few weeks later. I will always have very happy memories of all the good times and holidays we had spent together.

We left Scotland and hastily drove back to Blackpool to return the hired car, which by then had many more miles on the clock. We retrieved my newly repaired one, complete with a very expensive new head gasket. We finally arrived home at midnight, in time for a night's rest before the 9am hospital appointment for a cataract operation on my right eye the next morning, which thankfully was very successful.

The following spring, Krassy and I went to ski in Switzerland with Robert and family. We all had a wonderful time. I went as a spectator, as sadly I had to accept that my skiing days were over – I knew my ageing bones were beginning to object to such vigorous exertion. I was happy though to cook for the family in the chalet belonging to Daniel, a distant cousin. It was great to have such an enjoyable family time together, and I was happy to be surrounded by the magnificent mountains which my grandmother Elise had adored but sadly missed when she came across to live in the UK as a teenager. Her mother had died in childbirth having her younger brother, and an aunt had brought my grandmother up. Elise first worked as a children's nurse, later married my grandfather and lived with him in Scotland, going on to have ten children of her own.

Later that year I went to Newmarket with John on a three-day course on breeding thoroughbred horses for racing. I had been before and found it so interesting. I thought that as John was so gifted with the handling of all livestock and had recently purchased two thoroughbred broodmares of his own, it would be a golden opportunity to visit some of the top English Stallions and Studs in the Newmarket area. We attended the lectures given by leading equine vets, toured their laboratories and heard about the nutritionist's latest discoveries on the equine digestive system. They also covered grassland management and the best types of permanent pasture; stallions and covering; preparation of the pregnant mare; and how to deal with possible complications of foaling. We came away with the latest knowledge, not forgetting that a good stock-man has to know and understand his animals. They are all individuals, and their metabolisms can vary immensely.

John and I also went to Ireland to visit The Derby Sales where I had a young gelding to be sold. It was fascinating watching so many excellent thoroughbreds on parade, and listening to the amusing Irish patter that accompanied the sales talk. It was a proud moment for me when my horse was sold and later went on to do well.

2007 saw many changes – Krassy had the offer of a good job at a private boarding – school where he had often been employed. I thought that as there was a bungalow available there, it made sense for him to take up the offer and move in. It would save him time and petrol not having to travel to and fro, and he would be able to lead a more independent life in the privacy of his own home. He was not keen on the idea as he did not like cooking, but when the school offered him his main meals in term time it seemed to be the right decision, so Krassy left. I was sad to see him go but he has always continued to be part of the family and usually arrives for a meal or two at weekends and is always there to help with whatever jobs need doing.

We have always remained the very best of friends. Just before he moved out we spent a long weekend in Paris and visited many of the highlights, including The Notre Dame Cathedral, which I had enjoyed visiting once before. We left the UK at 4am, and my energy level had reached a very low ebb, so I sat in a pew while Krassy wandered round looking at all the finer details of the amazing architecture. I fell asleep and fortunately with my head bowed, people thought I was praying.

Well rested, we continued with a boat trip down the river, visited The Eiffel Tower, and managed to acquire two tickets for the famous Moulin Rouge Show which was packed out. It was fun to watch and a little risqué, the most memorable act was when we saw a very scantily clad lady in a bath full of snakes.

In 2008 I accompanied John, Lesley and her mother to France where they were to finalise the purchase of a farm. It was in an impressive area with a micro climate, and huge boulders of rock appearing every now and again in unexpected places. The farm situated near Secondigny, is approximately one hours drive from the sea on the west coast and twenty minutes from Parthenay, an interesting medieval town with a castle, steeped in ancient history, including interesting stories of resistance escapades, both from World War One and Two.

All went well and in 2009, they moved into the traditional French farmhouse with several barns and farm buildings surrounded by plenty of grazing land. They both worked very hard to transform it into a comfortable home. John took his farm machinery down and within six months had the farm up and running. His horses settled in to their new environment, and the nucleus of his new herd of Charolais Cattle was formed along with his Dorset Sheep.

I have been fortunate enough to visit them once or twice each year and have been able to watch the progress. John converted part of the farmhouse into an annex for Lesley's mother. She is great company and a bonus for me, as we are the same age and both originate from Surrey. The French neighbours are friendly and invite us for coffee. When I walk down the road anyone driving by gives a cheery wave as they all know who I am. It is a small village with an amazing grapevine when anyone new is in residence.

Lesley has been voted onto the commune council which she feels is an honour to be bestowed on an English person. I am sure they are lucky to have her as she has much to give the little community. In France, the councils maintain all the roads, verges and ditches that run alongside so everywhere looks very tidy. The country lanes look like a patchwork quilt as every pot-hole is repaired as soon as it becomes visible. Most of the small villages, which are few and far between, welcome all who pass through with decorative troughs growing seasonal flowers. Every nook and cranny has a splash of colour. It is impressive especially around the churches and village centres. They look as though they have been manicured, they are so smart. Most noticeable is the fact that there is no litter anywhere.

I love my visits to France; it is interesting to watch the fields of maize, sunflowers, wheat, oats, barley and other crops becoming more advanced as we head further south on the drive down. France is much more productive than I had realised. There are herds of various French bred cattle and sheep. I always feel quite at home once I am back there. Lesley is a wonderful cook so I don't have to think about preparing meals, just eating them, which is wonderful. I help to weed the garden in exchange and if it is raining, I enjoy chopping kindling wood, ready for lighting the wood burner in the winter. I help John in the mornings to muck out a large barn, which he cleverly converted into two parts for the thoroughbred horses, one of which I had bred. She was a daughter out of my brood mare, 'Kingsfold Blaze'. One half of the barn is for mares with foals, and the other half is for yearlings. It enables them to live more naturally and remain as a herd. They can see one another, but can run in and out to separate fields in the day time. John also designed some useful pens inside the barn, so any horses requiring special attention are all under the same roof. He also made some isolation boxes behind the cattle barns.

It is so peaceful down there; the moment I step out of the car the air feels clean and fresh. There is hardly any traffic, about one car or tractor an hour may pass by, and there are no aeroplanes. In the evenings when the sun sinks down, there is hardly a sound to be heard, except for the distant chime of the church clock marking the time, and the odd hooting of an owl. With stars twinkling up in the sky and the moon shining as it rises up from behind the trees, it is magical. First thing on a fine spring morning, I love to perch on a wall behind the barns and gaze out at the panoramic view of woods and fields with just one or two farm-houses way off in the distance. I let my whole being absorb the very essence of life around me, especially when the sky is bright blue and little puffs of cloud like cotton wool float by, and the trees are fresh and green, bursting into life. The birds herald in the new day with a dawn chorus full of mating calls, pigeons cooing, the hoop-poop of the noisy hoopoes and a cuckoo calling in the distance, while buzzards give an eerie call as they circle high in the sky. The cats slink cautiously back into the barn after a night's hunting, trying to avoid the sharp eyes of the dogs who are always keen to chase them.

In summer the smell of new-mown hay delights the nostrils and baby coypus emerge and swim from secret hidey-holes along the river bank as they come out to graze, often secretly observed by a kingfisher.

No hustle and bustle just Nature at her best, treasured moments indeed.

In 2010, Victoria my eldest granddaughter married Ben a charming local builder. Although the actual marriage ceremony took place in Horsham, family and friends were invited to celebrate at a coastal resort in Murcia, Spain, where Ben's parents have a holiday home. Most of the family and friends flew down but I thought that it would be a golden opportunity to motor down through France. Krassy was happy to drive, and keen to see Spain.

We visited John and Lesley on the way and then carried on down through the Pyrenees into Spain and followed the coast along. I had not visited that part of Spain before and found it most interesting seeing all the olives, oranges and lemons growing in such abundance.

Victoria had organised the celebration with great skill, every little detail had been perfectly planned. Many of the guests were booked into the same hotel and it was fun at breakfast the morning after we had arrived to find so many familiar faces from Horsham and the surrounding area.

Krassy bought a smart new shirt and tie just a couple of hours before the ceremony. His friend had christened him 'lastminute.com.' The hotel had an indoor balcony which surrounded the hall where the ceremony took place, which was exquisitely decorated throughout with flowers. Victoria looked gorgeous in her wedding dress and Ben and all the men wore special smart beige suites. Robert gave his daughter away and her Uncle Steven conducted the ceremony. A choir sang sweetly, and afterwards the reception took place in a restaurant on a little pier belonging to the hotel which jutted out over the sea. It was a fairytale wedding.

Two days later Krassy and I headed for Madrid and then up through Burgos to the north coast of Spain through Bilbao, San Sebastian and back into France to Biarritz. We stopped off at several places, especially in the picturesque little coves where the forests went down to the sea. The people were friendly and although we did not speak any Spanish we managed, except for just a few problems at the self service petrol stations where there was no attendant to help. On one occasion the machine gobbled up my debit card. When we pressed the help button the lady who answered did not speak English, which was difficult, but luckily a few minutes later the machine spat my card back at me, having taken the correct amount of money, which was a great relief.

Once back in France we watched grapes being harvested with the help of the latest technology, no longer picked by hand. Instead massive, specially designed tractors knock the grapes off and collect them in a huge hopper. The vineyard belonged to a family – Grandfather, Father and Grandson – who were all very busy, but once they realised how interested we were in the whole procedure, we were lucky enough to be taken back to the farm and were able to see the whole process. The grandson was a well educated gentleman who spoke excellent English, he kindly found the time and was proud to show us round,

We called in at a couple of distilleries and saw champagne in the making and were fortunate to find somewhere to stay in a small hotel, which appeared to be miles from anywhere. It happened to be owned by a French entertainer who was quite famous. There were no other guests that night and, primed with a glass or two of brandy, he serenaded us with his French songs. He gave us a CD of his music and an invitation to his next concert in Paris, which sadly time did not allow us to attend. It was a most unexpected, thrilling climax to the holiday and we felt that we had been lucky that he had been in residence at the time of our stay.

We called in to see John and Lesley on the way home, they were happy to hear details of the wedding and our other exploits. Once we reached the English coastline, it was interesting to be welcomed home by seagulls again, as their absence had been noticeable at the other coastal resorts we had visited.

In the autumn of 2013, I went up to Scotland with Robert on a business trip and introduced him to Scottish relations that he had never met. It was fascinating to see how alike they were in build. Linda and her family made us very welcome. Robert had a good look round St. Andrews and Donald, who is a harbour master around the coast, took us on a tour of the harbour to see fish, prawns and crabs being sorted and Leonard took us up in the haunted tower at Pittenweem where they had once kept and tortured witches, before they were burned at the stake. He is very interested in the local history and has published several books on the subject. The tortured were innocent victims, one a distant relative. It was creepy, even more so when we learned more of the barbaric and terrible practices that had occurred in that tower. Similar horrific events

217

have been recorded well into the seventeen hundreds throughout much of Europe. The tower at Pittenweem is open to visitors.

Largo, which is nearby, is where the story of Robinson Crusoe originated. Alexander Selkirk was his real name before Daniel Defoe transformed him into the legend we know today. The real story is that a fight ensued between Alexander and his brother who had offered him a glass of water. Alexander had arrived home from a voyage having had a dram too much to drink. The glass was full of sea water which he hastily spat out, and was furious at being made the laughing stock of the family. The fight eventually became a family brawl. Alexander was supposed to have appeared in court for violent behaviour, but instead he went off to sea. He fell out with the Captain of the ship who left him on the island to teach him a lesson, thinking that he would be picked up by a passing ship in a week or two. It actually took four years before he was rescued and returned home.

I think Robert was suitably impressed with St. Andrews the capital of The Kingdom Of Fife, and home of many of his often feuding forefathers, which as well as being renowned for its famous golf course also has many treasured tales to fire the imagination.

Shortly after we had arrived home from our trip to Scotland, Robert and I shared a proud moment with Krassy when we witnessed him become a British Citizen. It was an interesting ceremony finishing with everyone present singing, 'God Save the Queen'.

That evening we went for a celebration supper, accompanied by the friend who had introduced Krassy to us in the first place.

John at 13 years with
Tara and Ricky, 1973

My Mum and Dad, late 1960s.

Robert's car and Ricky on
Paddy, 1972.

Horses at Wattlehurst,
1982
Doodle with Flash,
Wind Jammer with Bonny,
Kate with Lisa

John with foal and David
with Lisa, 1970.

Ricky aged 4 mending his trike

John and Ricky on a tandem bike John made, 1970.

John's first buggy he made from his old car, 1972.

Robert, David and John sorting the car out

John with the tractor he fitted with dual wheels to go through wet ground

Ricky with his first bulldozer

The Nyes at the front of the house. Robert, David, George, John and Ricky

Christmas 1981 in big room

Jane, Tara, Shep and Correy, 1980.

The blue merles with cat in the kitchen, 1980s

Kingsfold Flame after winning a
big race, me leading her in, 1980s.

Flashing Steel at 3 days old.
Born up at Wattlehurst in the
early 1980s. Won the 1995
Irish Grand National

Flashing Steel – R Dunwoody, winning Novice Series Final, Fairyhouse,
Feb 1993

Youngsters, me checking them over, 2005.

*Blaze, with her one
day old foal, 2007.*

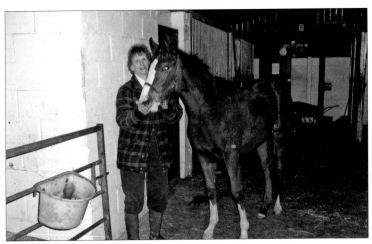

Me with promising youngster in new stables, 2002.

Fred with Tiger as a puppy.

Always look after your terrier,
Protect him from wet and from cold,
For the love of a dog for his master,
Just can not be measured in gold.

Fred with Tiger his beloved hunt terrier, 1992

Fred and me at a posh do, 1992

Fred with his daffodils, early 1990s

Freds daffodils.
My dad with his girlfriend Betty,
both lived into their nineties, 1998.

*My cousin Mariette
in Canada when
we went to see her
brothers, 1994*

*Refurbishing
my bungalow.
Tessa inspecting,
2004.*

*Refurbishing
my bungalow,
almost finished.
Tessa waiting
for a tit-bit,
2004.*

My new conservatory and rescued plants, 2008.

New potting house greenhouse and path. Krassy built from old green houses and unwanted scraps, 2006.

Rescued plants. Krassy made the stepping stone path, 2007.

Grandchildren

Victoria and Amanda with shelties.

Debbie and Simon with Laura.

Rex

Kim, Sam with little Sprite and Oliver.

Harry and Max.

My 80th birthday cake. 20th April 2013

Stella, Me and Ena. My old school friends at my 80th Birthday party.

My 80th Birthday party. Me with most of my grandchildren

People watching. Just enjoying the ambience in Saumur, France 2013.

Sun, sea and sand. Krassy and me on The Scilly Isles.

Krassy's first van and Tessa on long drive up to "Wattlehurst"
(white speck seen in middle of the photo).

Krassy and me at Blair Castle on a Scottish tour, 2000

Krassy and me on Lily the elephant in the jungle on Samui Island 2014
Cruise to the Far East

CHAPTER 32

80 Years Young

In the Spring of 2013, Lynne and Ricky suggested that I may like to have a special party in April to celebrate my milestone 80th birthday. They kindly offered their home as the venue, and also to make all the arrangements for the event. It was a lovely surprise and I happily accepted. Lynne suggested I make a list of friends whom I would like to invite. The numbers began to grow and with the help of my Christmas list it grew even bigger until it reached just over fifty; several more than first envisaged. Lynne and Ricky were unfazed, and Lynne designed a unique invitation card complete with photos of me on the front and a piece of raffia to decorate and hold it together. The invitations were sent out several weeks before the event and to my amazement almost all were accepted.

Not being one for dressing up I thought the smart casual look would be quite suitable, so I decided on the comfortable blue jersey suit that Lynne and Ricky had given me for Christmas. The plans were underway.

The weather had been quite cold and unsettled leading up to the event, but on my birthday I awoke to a beautiful blue sky and as the sun rose I could see I was going to be blessed with an amazing warm sunny spring day. I visited my hairdresser Theresa in the morning and she gave my hair a look of unaccustomed glamour, no longer the usual spectacle I wore, that of looking as though I had been dragged through a hedge backwards!

Lynne, Ricky, Harry and Max had made all the preparations. I arrived just as Lynne's Mother was putting delicate finishing touches to the beautiful flower arrangements with which she had decorated the house.

The garden had been manicured and looked an absolute picture. As the guests began to arrive, Ricky greeted them at the door and grandsons Harry and Max served drinks as they entered while I welcomed them.

I so enjoyed seeing everyone from the different areas of my life chatting away merrily together, and my grandchildren greeting their cousins – a cluster of young adults in a corner enjoying the get together. I was thrilled when they all lined up outside for a photo call with me in the centre, a photo which I will always treasure, along with the many others that were taken. Max put them all on a memory stick for me before I went home.

It was a memorable occasion indeed: family including Krassy, many friends, some of whom I had not seen for ages, my sister, old school friends, dog racing and horsey friends, and old farming friends reminiscing over the years at Wattlehurst. Many of my market colleagues managed to make it too. Also present were evening class students and even some from my latest 'writing a book' class, responsible for actually inspiring me to keep writing it all down.

A large table was beautifully laid out with the most magnificent spread including a huge bowl of my favourite succulent king prawns; I have to admit that I helped quite a few to disappear. The large homemade birthday cake stood in pride of place on a table by itself. When it was time to cut it, Ricky carefully carried it outside and placed it on a table in prime position, where everyone was sitting around enjoying the warm sunshine. Ricky gave a little speech and I followed by thanking Ricky and Lynne for organising my party, and all my guests for coming and making it such a special occasion for me. Everybody sang 'Happy Birthday', accompanied by Max on the piano, before devouring the delicious cake.

Gradually the guests departed and my sister and I were among the last to leave.

I will always treasure my 80th birthday party memories – what a day!

CHAPTER 33

Confucius He Say Go On Cruise!

Krassy and I had often mused about going on a cruise together. Years before I had daydreamed about cruising round the world. However, having reached 80 years old I thought perhaps I was leaving it a little late. One evening when Krassy came in for supper, I asked him if he was still interested in going on a cruise. He jumped at the idea and as it was just after Christmas, when outside work was often curtailed by the weather, it was a good time for both of us to take a break. I just wanted to go somewhere I had never been before that was a contrast to life in Europe. Krassy was keen on going to the Far East, inspired by the stories he had seen on films as a boy about the Vietnamese War. Destination agreed, we started to look on the internet for the best last minute deals.

After hunting around we found just what we were looking for on a Holland American cruise liner named 'The Volandam'. It was sailing half way round the world but took passengers on and off at various locations. She was due to arrive and cruise from Hong Kong down the coast of Vietnam, Cambodia, Thailand and down to Malaysia, docking at various places en route. It really was a last minute deal. We just had time to top up our injections and sort out travel insurance before we flew out to meet her in Hong Kong Harbour.

Robert kindly took us to Heathrow where we boarded one of British Airways latest planes. The captain proudly announced that it was an A380 and barely a year old. The flight took over eleven hours but we were wined and dined and given cold drinks through the night. I watched a few comedy programmes on my small individual TV screen and was fascinated to watch the plane's flight path and identify the countries we were passing over. I slept on and off. In the morning we circled over Hong Kong waiting to land and had an amazing birds-eye view of the harbour, which was surrounded by hundreds of skyscrapers.

Once safely back on terra firma, we taxied along the runway into a very busy, bustling Hong Kong airport. It was the Chinese New Year and everywhere was adorned with bright flowers, welcoming passengers and encouraging them to join in and celebrate the various festivities. Mock dragons were parading around the airport. We took a taxi and were amazed at all the skyscrapers towering above us as we toured round Hong Kong on the way to the docks.

Once at the harbour, the 'Volandam' loomed up in front of us, a huge majestic cruiser.

A surge of excitement sparked through me and I had to pinch myself to realise that it was really happening as we boarded. After the security checks we felt very grand when we mingled with the other passengers and investigated our new surroundings, which were quite lavish. There were nine levels altogether with lifts, which every day displayed the day and date on the mats on the floor, as it is easy to lose all sense of time while on board. There were hand washes at all levels, a theatre and two swimming pools, one inside and the other out on the sunbathing deck, complete with a huge supply of clean towels and a bar to help quench the thirst. There were tennis courts, a gym, beauty parlour and lots of places to eat. Some restaurants were very expensive, but we preferred to use the excellent 24 hour self-service restaurant, which was completely replenished every few hours. Room service was also available on request. The food was excellent with a choice of American, English, Italian, Chinese, Japanese, Indian and more. Everywhere was spotless with a high regard to cleanliness in all areas.

Later on that first evening on board, there was a spectacular laser light display which lit up the coast around Hong Kong, all part of the celebrations for the Chinese New Year. At the end of the day we were both ready to catch up on sleep and did not surface until 10am the next day, to discover we were sailing down the Vietnamese coast to Hanoi. We spent the day sunbathing and carefully planned and booked the various coach trips which we had chosen to take en route. In the evening after watching the theatre show, we ventured up into The Crows Nest on the top deck where we joined an American couple and many of the slightly older generation who were letting their hair down at the bar where dancing was in progress. We met people of all nationalities; American, Dutch, Australian, Chinese and Japanese but not many from the UK. Wherever they had come from, they were all very friendly.

The next morning all coach trippers had an early start. The theatre was the assembly point and as we entered we were given a coloured number to stick on our shirts depicting which coach tour we were on. We waited until our number was announced, then everyone was checked off the boat before boarding the coaches. We proceeded outside to find a fleet of various coloured, air-conditioned vehicles with an English speaking guide awaiting their passengers. It was all efficiently organised.

Our first tour was to see the highlights of Hanoi. It was an interesting three and a half hour journey each way and was to be an eleven-hour day. We passed through many villages and markets, stopping off every now and again. Once in Hanoi, Vietnam's capital city, we visited The Ho Chi Min quarter and learnt that there were over 15 million people living in the city. After a walk through the ancient streets it was not difficult to believe that it was true. It was full of old world charm with people buzzing like bees in a hive, many trying to sell their wares. The very essence of Vietnamese culture was alive. At some of the shrines that we visited we were asked to remove our shoes and leave them at the door. We had been warned on the boat to keep an eye on them as children often took them and demanded a ransom for their return. We went on to visit the One Pillar Pagoda and stepped inside The Temple of Literature, Vietnam's first university built in 1070 and dedicated to Confucius.

The next day we spent on the boat recovering from our foray into Hanoi, while we gracefully cruised on to DA Nang. Our next trip was to visit The Imperial City of the Nguyen Emperors, passing through the impressive Mon gate to the Imperial Citadal and on to the ornate Palace of Supreme Harmony and the Pavilion of Benevolence. We visited some ancient tombs and I was intrigued to see some wild monkeys playing on the other side of a tranquil lake.

On our rest days between trips we swam and relaxed on the boat in the hot and humid conditions as we cruised further south down the coast.

Nha Trang was our next stop. We visited the Po Nagar Cham Towers which were built between the 7th and 12th centuries by the ancient Cham civilization. We crossed the Xom Bong Bridge and enjoyed the colourful view of fishing boats moored in the picturesque harbour. Sadly, much of the water in many places we visited was choked up with plastic of all descriptions floating along the edges and we witnessed the unhealthy haze of pollution drifting over some of the more heavily populated areas. The people seemed happy with their lives; mobile phones were much in evidence and small motor cycles were everywhere, often with two adults with small children sandwiched between them on board. Crash helmets had recently been made compulsory, and had dramatically reduced the accident rate. We continued on to the Long Son Pagoda with 152 stone steps up to view the giant white Buddha. I stayed at the bottom while Krassy climbed up all the steps to take photographs. We shopped in a market and stopped off at one of the large art complexes where many pieces of artwork were for sale. We watched young girls making them, some of whom were incredibly beautiful. The articles too, including silk clothing, were exquisite.

On all our coach excursions we stopped for lunch and were welcomed at the most elegant hotels where the food was excellent.

Our next destination was Phu My, where the famous Chu Chi tunnels were. After a three hour drive we entered what had been a war zone of incredible strategic importance. A military guide joined us and after a short film we went on a guided tour and learned how the guerrilla fighters operated, and how they had lived and fought underground in the tunnels. Krassy was in his element when he went underground and crawled through one. It was told from the Vietnamese perspective and must have been a poignant moment for some of our former American Army passengers who had actually fought in the Vietnamese War.

It is difficult to understand why human beings have to behave in such a manner. Mr Gould, my old headmaster, taught us that History was true stories from the past which repeated themselves over and over and over again, especially when it came to war – lessons were never learned. I think that the ancient Chinese Philosopher Lao Tsu, who was an older contemporary of Confucius and a keeper of the imperial archives at Loyang in the province of Honan in the sixth century BC, had a sensible philosophy with his idea of Taoism. He wrote many words of wisdom, including:

The more laws and restrictions there are,
The poorer people become,
The sharper men's weapons,
The more trouble in the land,
The more ingenious and clever men are,
The more strange things happen,
The more rules and regulations,
The more thieves and robbers.

I came across his 5,000 word book of TAO TE CHING at a car-boot sale in the UK and bought it for a pound. I have always found the ancient far eastern concept of life fascinating. It has been so interesting to actually see where it all originated.

I was also interested in what Confucius had to say, especially his saying 'The man takes a drink. The drink takes a drink. Then the drink takes the man'!

Sihanoukville in Cambodia was our next port of call. We enjoyed a two hour countryside drive to Kampot Town. On the way we saw acres of paddy fields where the rice was sown and learnt how and why the fields were flooded during part of the growing process. We visited a pepper plantation which produced some of the best peppers in the world. The farmers were friendly as we witnessed their daily lives, many selling their produce. I bought enough black peppers to last me a lifetime. A lady was splitting coconuts and I drank some of the delicious, sweet milk from them. We congregated around the rubber trees and watched the sticky sap, oozing out where the bark had been stripped off, then we were shown how it was transformed into the rubber we recognised. It was a very educational visit.

We had lunch in the French colonial town of Kampot. It was strange to see French style houses in Cambodia. Later we visited the fishing village of Ropan Popov, and strolled through the neighbourhood. I was alarmed to see groups of young children, maybe only three or four years old, running barefoot through the rubbish, much of it plastic. They seemed happy enough and liked to say 'Hello', in English. Some of them followed us down to the water's edge where the harbour was packed with boats of all shapes and sizes with noticeably lots more rubbish floating in the water between them. The fish markets were fascinating. We saw so many strange fish of all different shapes and sizes on display. I was amused when I saw a motor bike pass by full of loose, unwrapped fish – possibly on the menu for supper – wobbling about in its pannier.

At Laem Chabang in Thailand we anchored for two days. Many of the passengers travelled into Bangkok, some had booked a hotel room for the night. I spent the first day on board, relaxing and managed to catch up with washing soiled clothes in the latest, do it yourself laundering facilities. It was so quick and the dryer was amazing. It circulated the wet washing in a huge drum and it all blew dry in just a few minutes. There were ironing facilities too.

The next day we visited The Sriracha Tiger Zoo, which was set in over a hundred acres of land, and home to over 200 Bengal tigers as well as 100,000 crocodiles. It was amazingly clean and tidy and all the animals were very well cared for, they looked a picture of good health. Many of the tiger cubs were hand reared, so they grew up being accustomed to humans. Visitors were allowed to bottle feed them for a small fee. Meanwhile the Tiger mothers appeared to be happy to rear a litter of little piglets instead. I fed a baby tiger, and also stroked and had my photo taken with a fully grown one. At the end of an amazing Tiger show, one of the tigers stood up with its paws on the trainer's shoulders, they were face to face with one another on friendly terms. There were several men in the ring who were keeping an eye on a dozen or so who were fully grown, well trained performing tigers. They all appeared to be contented and happy; certainly much safer than the wild ones, who are so often preyed upon by poachers. The crocodiles were amazing, there were so many, sunbathing in and beside the pool. The show was unbelievable. A young couple coaxed a crocodile to open its mouth wide, then in turn actually put their head into the animals gaping jaws, between all its carnivorous, pointed teeth. The crowd was aghast at the performance.

The elephant show was clever too. They played football, scoring goals and performing remarkable balancing acts. At the end they paraded past the visitors waving their trunks over into the crowd foraging for tit-bits, some people offered fruit, which they ate, but if it was paper money they took it with their trunk, then dutifully passed it to their keepers.

In the evening we watched some of the Volandam, crew releasing the ropes which held the massive cruise liner along the quayside, then the loud clanking noise of the mighty anchor being retracted. We watched as we gracefully sailed out of the harbour accompanied by two pilot boats which saw us safely on our way.

The next morning we had arrived at Koh Samui Island which belongs to Thailand where we were driven by four wheel drive vehicles on a Jungle Eco Safari. We passed through some villages and stopped to watch the local tradition of a trained monkey climbing high up a tree to pluck and throw down the coconuts. We went further into the jungle and the highlight of the trip for me was when we had a long ride on Lily, a thirty-one year old elephant. She was gorgeous and very well behaved. It made a pleasant change from driving on the M25 back home.

We spent our last day on board resting before we disembarked. The next morning, it was sad when we had to leave the Volandam. It had given us a wonderful holiday. Over night she had arrived in Singapore harbour which is in Malaysia. Once we had disembarked, our luggage was stored in the coach while we spent the morning touring round and were amazed at the contrast between many of the other places we had visited, where a large percentage of living conditions were very basic, and then in Singapore which oozed affluence, everywhere looked so prosperous. We were told that many of the houses there cost millions of pounds.

We visited The Royal Orchid Gardens which were spectacular, they had an amazing collection of orchids, and the rest of the gardens were so well kept and colourful. Then it was off to the airport ready for our long flight home. The coach dropped us at the main entrance where decorations for the Chinese New Year were still in evidence. There were beautiful flowers everywhere and because it was the year of the horse, a huge model of one stood near the entrance also surrounded by flowers. The Fairy Tale Holiday had come to an end. It was time to come down to earth again.

Later in the evening we boarded our plane for the UK. After thirteen hours we arrived back at Heathrow where Robert met us and drove us home. We dropped Krassy off, ready for work the next day. I would not have had such a great time if it had not been for him, he helped me so much, his arm invaluable when we had to climb so many steps when we visited the various shrines. We never had a cross word. I was lucky in the fact that he has always had a great respect for the older generation. I had found it quite touching to see him with my Father, also when we visited a couple of my uncles who were all well into their nineties. He treated them with great reverence, amazed that they had reached such a great age. He had commented a few years earlier when my age was catching up with me that he would be happy to push me in my wheelchair but would stop short of changing my pampers!

It seemed strange being back home again. It is good to realise how lucky we are in so many respects when you see how little some people the other side of the world have to live on. Yet they seemed perfectly happy, something that money cannot buy.

CHAPTER 34

Reflections.......

Looking back on my life there have been many ups and downs. There are so many highlights, including the breeding and rearing of many successful racing greyhounds, including two puppy derby winners. Once I had graduated into thoroughbred horses, I was fortunate enough to have bred and reared several top class winners and placed horses, the most thrilling moment being when I learnt that Flashing Steel had won The 1995 Irish Grand National.

And of course, most importantly, with the help of George's genes I bred and reared four wonderful sons. The boys, now all in their fifties survived their rough but ready upbringing, and with credit to George's "get up and go" genes, inherited plenty of drive and initiative. They have all done well in their lives.

The family has now increased. To date, I have nine wonderful grandchildren, four girls and five boys, two step-grandchildren two great-grandsons and one great-granddaughter. It is so fascinating to me observing how various family traits and mannerisms continue down through the generations.

It has been a privilege to share several strong friendships over the years, and one of life's most valuable lessons must be to appreciate the enormous worth of true friendship.

My old school friend Ena has been, and remains, an especially loyal friend over many years. Our families have gone their separate ways, but we still all come together for special events and to reminisce, remembering all the happy and sometimes sad times we have shared together.

Regularly my phone rings and it's Ena. A typical conversation goes something like this one from a few years ago

"Hello Brenda how are you? Would you like to come to the NFU coach trip next week? "

"Yes I'd love to. What time and where are we going?"

"We'll pick you up at six o'clock and we're going dog racing down at Hove. See you then," says Ena.

"OK. Look forward to it," I replied.

The trip to Hove was fun, meeting up with friends from what was always, 'The Young Farmers' Club', but is now referred to as 'The Old Farmers' Club', with chats about the state of our health and happy memories of days gone by.

"How's your arthritis?"

"When is your hip replacement? Oh, you've had your knees done already!"

"What happened to Gloria in the end, did she marry that chap with the beard?"

"Do you remember when we were in the netball team at school? Those cream teas afterwards?"

"I'll never forget when Don decided to blow up that old concrete pillbox left over from the war. Do you remember the fun we had stuffing it up with clay while he sorted out the detonator? How we were well out of the way when it blew up?"

"I remember giving your Dad and Uncle John a haircut. They just wanted a trim, it was my first try and it definitely became a little more than a trim!"

"Yes, it just seems like yesterday," nods Ena, leaning on her walking stick. "How's your back?"

"Oh, the Doctor says it's wear and tear, some discs have gone. In other words he reckons I'm just about worn out. If I was a horse, the next stop would be the knackers yard! However, I'm very relieved that's not the case. I'm waiting for the clever medical scientists to perfect the latest stem cell therapies, so I live in hope and in the meantime I can enjoy all my true lifelong friends and wonderful happy memories!"

THE END

Acknowledgements

I have so enjoyed writing this book, although it has taken five years typing with one finger (occasionally two!), of twisting and twirling the words in my attempt to untangle them and set them down in grammatically correct English. The poems however come to you just as they came from my head, complete with misrelated participles!

I originally started to the write the book for future generations of my family who may be interested one day to learn a little of their family history and to know more about how life was for their older relatives and ancestors before TV, computers, mobile phones and the wonder of the electronic world wide web.

It has been cathartic sitting quietly and allowing the memories of my life to slowly filter through my mind. At least should I sadly succumb to the dreaded dementia, there will be a record of where I have been and what I have done.

I have so many people to thank for their help in the production of this book, really too many to mention, but the support of family and friends throughout my project has been greatly appreciated. I have to name just some of them individually. So thank you to:

Dr Claudia Gould and the Horsham "Writing a Book" group who kept me focussed and gave me continuous feedback.

Angela, Peter, Roy and Kevin, thank you for your patient contributions.

Justine and her Mother Mary for reading my finished draft and offering very worthwhile suggestions.

Pam and her husband Ted, who proofread and gave valuable advice.

Petra, who took the time to proofread and offered ideas and encouragement.

My good friend Gill who has been with me from the start, checking grammar, motivating and helping me in exchange for bowls of homemade soup!

Debbie, who read my drafts along the way and offered ideas and kind words sometimes from afar!

Lynne, who has supported me over many years with kindness. Her understanding of my difficult times gave her a unique ability to contribute to the book, and I hope her suggestion that I write an honest account of my experience will prove helpful to others who find themselves in similar circumstances.

Lesley, who helped me enormously, guiding me through the maze of actually producing and printing the published book.

I couldn't have done it without any of you!

I really can't believe it
I have actually grown old
No longer super fighting fit
And prone to feeling cold!

Tally-Ho – the vixen's gone to earth!